To Vera Brown and Scott Brown

We did it!

I love you.

I miss you.

Thank you.

THE PRETTY ONE

ON LIFE,
POP CULTURE, DISABILITY,
AND OTHER REASONS TO FALL IN LOVE WITH ME

KEAH BROWN

ATRIA PAPERBACK

New York London Toronto Sydney New Delhi

ATRIA PAPERBACK

An Imprint of Simon & Schuster, Inc.
1230 Avenue of the Americas
New York, NY 10020

Copyright © 2019 by Keah Brown

First Atria Paperback edition August 2019

ATRIA PAPERBACK and colophon are trademarks of Simon & Schuster, Inc.

For information about special discounts for bulk purchases, please contact Simon & Schuster Special Sales at 1-866-506-1949 or business@simonandschuster.com.

The Simon & Schuster Speakers Bureau can bring authors to your live event. For more information or to book an event, contact the Simon & Schuster Speakers Bureau at 1-866-248-3049 or visit our website at www.simonspeakers.com.

Interior design by Laura Levatino

Manufactured in the United States of America

1   3   5   7   9   10   8   6   4   2

Library of Congress Cataloging-in-Publication Data has been applied for.

ISBN 978-1-9821-0054-4
ISBN 978-1-9821-0055-1 (ebook)

THE PRETTY ONE

CONTENTS

....

INTRODUCTION

Hey, friends! My name is Keah and I'm cute as hell. I love popular culture, music, cheesecake, cheeseburgers, and pizza. I dance in cars with my friends and again at their weddings. We sing songs down store aisles and play cards for hours. I live-tweet TV shows and laugh at my own jokes. I text my friend Danielle Sepulveres about Christmas movies and watch the Hallmark Channel for hours. When I am alone, I thoroughly enjoy playing *The Sims*. I am obsessed with lipsticks and I am trying and failing to learn the art of applying eye shadow. (I hope that you read all of that in the same vein as the intro to the Nickelodeon show *The Wild Thornberrys*, because that was my intent, though I don't think it lines up quite as nicely as I would have liked it to.)

My point is that I do all these things in a disabled body, not because I am *brave* or *bold*, but because I like doing them and I would love doing them in any body. I adapt to the world because I have to do so in order to live. My disability is cerebral palsy, and it affects the right side of my body, effectively altering my motor skills and reaction time as well as the strength of my bones on that side. I don't do things in spite of anything—except for maybe the people who told me I'd be nothing and no one. I don't mind being an inspiration if it is for a valid reason, such as admiring how many slices of pizza I ate, an essay or an article I wrote, my clothing choices, or how quickly I can learn the lyrics to songs. As long as the inspiration doesn't come with pity or self-congratulatory pats on the back, I am all for it. Let my love for cheesecake inspire you the way it will one day inspire a nation. At least you can say you were there first.

Before I hop on a soapbox, let me stop and share some fun but key facts about myself. Let's start with music: Paramore and Demi Lovato are my favorite musicians, and music has been a huge part of my journey so far. I tell myself that my love for TV is balanced only by my love for books, so it's fitting that I became a writer, in order to write about TV and fight for proper representation in media for people who look like me, and a journalist, in order to talk to musicians, writers, and actors. I love doing both, so don't even bother asking me to choose. I like getting lost in other people's worlds for a while—it takes the pressure off having to answer for my disabled body and sit in the contempt that some people have for it—and I like talking to people and figuring out how and why they became who they became. I hate winter even though I live in western New York, where it snows so much that it has felt like a personal attack on my life, for all my life.

Apart from the weather where I live, my life experience is far exceeding my expectations. I never thought anyone would want to hear what I had to say until I started telling stories and talking about the things and people that matter to me. The truth is this: I've always felt average, plain, and wrong, but there is nothing average, plain, or wrong about me, and it took me only half my life so far to figure that out. I wrote an entire book and you are gearing up to read it. How cool is that? So cool.

Sometimes, it is beautiful to prove yourself wrong.

A thing that happens when you're tasked with writing a book is that you start to learn new things about yourself while you write to contend with your past. Who I am at present is a person who loudly and proudly gives a damn about herself, other people, and the world at large. Caring is fun, and I find that it has made me both happier and healthier, though I wish that I could care less about the opinions of naysayers. Rome wasn't built in a day and all that, so I'm guessing there is still time to change and reach my final form. When writing this book, I had to remind myself that who I had been in the past is important, too, and I try my hardest to remember that, instead of hiding her away out of embarrassment. In any case, I am unable to go back in time and tell her what I think she knows now. If I did that, though, who knows if any of this would still be possible? I won't let wishful time travel get in the way of my experience.

There is still so much left to learn. One of the biggest things that I am discovering is that I should learn to sit in my joy longer and not immediately apologize for being proud and happy. My happiness and joy are still relatively new because I started embracing them only four years ago, and while they are still growing, changing, and taking form in new and exciting ways, where I am now and where I am going are possible only because of where I was.

What I can see now is that I was always cute. I look at old pictures and see a girl whose smile was wide and face was full but who didn't see her beauty. I smiled widely for a girl who didn't like waking up and seeing herself, because she didn't want anyone else to know the truth, which she let out only when she was alone. It is my belief that sometimes we keep secrets and hide our deepest insecurities because we believe that if other people found them out they would agree and believe them to be true, too. At least, this was why I tried my hardest not to let on how depressed and angry I was. (But I'm certain now that I wasn't as good at hiding my feelings as I thought I was.)

At the time, I didn't recognize that I was feeding into the narrative of shame and disability that society had created: that Keah saw someone so broken that she could never be whole again. Yes, my insecurities were self-made, but they had been encouraged and influenced by a society that had taught me early on that I was not supposed to feel beautiful in a body like mine. I was supposed to hate it until the day I died. The minute I stopped listening to that kind of thinking was the minute I started living.

I am a twenty-six-year-old black woman with a physical disability who is much more than her disability. However, I understand that the erasure of disability in our society is just as harmful as the negative portrayals of disability throughout our society. For a really long time I believed that ignoring my disability and tucking it into the deepest parts of myself would make it go away. But that isn't the way the world works, and that is no way to live. My disability is not a thing to see past but instead a thing to acknowledge and accept before able-bodied people and I continue existing at the same time in this world. I have both physical and invisible disabilities, and I refuse to be ashamed of them, because they are beautiful in their uniqueness and their familiarity. They are mine, but they also belong to a world of others, and that makes them worthy of my appreciation and acceptance.

When I sat down to write this collection, I decided that honesty would be the basis of the essays you will read. Honesty in the face of sadness, imperfection, anger, grief, and joy. Now that I have joy, I never want to let it go. I want to smother it like a middle-aged mother who is sending her son off to college or a father who lingers at the door after his child has left for her very first date—until his wife softly pats him on the arm before pulling him away. (I watch a lot of Hallmark movies, as I said, where these things happen, so just go with it.) I find that in order for me to be the best version of myself, these stories have to be told, because I need to forgive myself for who I was in order to become who I am becoming. The saying goes that no idea is original but that the people who share the idea and stories are—that has to count for something, right? Black disabled women aren't the ones you see on store bookshelves; we aren't the ones you catch at literary events and on bestseller lists. I want to change that, and the best way I know how is through the written word. I write to feel seen and heard. I write so that I cannot be ignored. My words are my announcement that I am here—and that I am not going anywhere.

These stories must live on in printed pages so that I can keep the people in them forever, so that when I am gone no one will be able to say that Keah Brown did not choose to live a life she was proud of. I am a black woman with cerebral palsy who loves herself *now*, and most days that feels like a revolutionary act. It took a lot of work to get to this place, a fountain of tears, grief, and loss, but I'm here, and it is beautiful.

I think in order to get where we are going I've got some bases to cover. When this book is first released into the world, I will be twenty-seven, and that's a big deal to me. First, because I am terrible at math and my twin sister had to tell me that we would not be twenty-eight when these words are first read. (This was bittersweet news, because a thing to know about me is that even numbers are my jam. They've been so good to me. Some of the most monumental things that have happened to me involved even numbers. I went to San Diego Comic-Con in 2014 with my friends and saw Paramore and Fall Out Boy in concert, and in 2016 I learned to love my body and the person in it. A year later, when I was twenty-six, I went viral after creating #DisabledAndCute, a hashtag that began as a celebration of that newfound love, and then I landed an agent and a book deal in the same year. I'm flexing a little, but these are the best examples I have.) Who knows where I will be when both you and I read these words bound in book form? But wherever I am, know that I am grateful and excited to share these stories of my life and the world around me with you.

The real star here, though, is #DisabledAndCute, my firstborn child. I had her on February 12, 2017, at 12:48 p.m. She weighed . . . I won't do that to you. You know how parents say they don't have a favorite child and that they love all their children equally? I believe it, but I also believe that there's special care and attention that comes with the first. My hashtag means the world to me and this book does, too, so I try hard to give them equal love and attention. I think it's working. At least when it comes to the hashtag and the book. In my human family, I refer to myself as the second firstborn, and I believe I am my mother's favorite—but that's another story. We should get back to the hashtag before my brother and sister learn the truth.

I didn't create my hashtag in the hopes that it would go viral and change my life, but that's exactly what happened. A celebration of myself became a place of community in which people from all walks of life began celebrating themselves and each other. The hashtag has given me the opportunity to speak in places like Portland, Oregon, and Greencastle, Indiana, about ethics, representation, and my hopes for the future. The hashtag has given me a place to belong and a thing to hold on to during the rough days while also helping me build an audience to get my other work in front of willing eyes and ears.

I dream of a life in which someone loves me romantically and in which I can attend my ten-year high school reunion with enough success to make everyone who doubted me jealous. (This is an admittedly silly dream that would feel a bit like the reunion in *Romy and Michele's High School Reunion*, except I wouldn't be lying about the Post-its but would absolutely keep the ending dance number.) Yet remember what I said about honesty. I did also dream of writing this book, *and I did it*, so literally anything and everything else feels possible now. The lesson I am learning in this life is that people give a damn much more than we might think possible.

Right now, I live in a city famous only for its locks along the Erie Canal. I live here with my mother, Cheryl; my twin sister, Leah; and my brother, Eric; as well as my aunts, cousins, and uncles. I live here while I dream of living in Los Angeles and calling the sunny locale my home. Before I turn that dream into reality, I spend too much time in Walmart, TJ Maxx, and Rue 21 for anyone's comfort. I attend sporadic game nights at my friend Demetrius's house. And I buy clothes online when I am having a bad day and need a pick-me-up. I live in a place of comfort that is all I have ever known, but I am ready to leave it for new adventures, knowing that I'll always have the people to come back to even when the home is no longer where it was.

My writing practices are routine. I write and interview people while sitting on my bed. I watch TV there, too, and I fall in love with fictional characters and make up scenarios to keep myself from feeling unlovable. I have a character or characters whom I love for every day of the week, depending on the show I'm watching that day. I love these characters—some romantically and some like you might love a puppy or a small child. In my real life, though, there is a bit of irony in knowing that I love myself even though someone else hasn't yet chosen to. The kind of love that I want now is of the romantic variety. I have more love from my friends and family than I have deserved sometimes. We don't have perfect relationships, of course; we still fight and yell and hurt each other the way you do as human beings, but the love is loud and unchanging. My friends and family loved me first, before any success I have had, before any partnerships with clothing companies or TV spots, and before I loved or liked myself. In many ways, this collection of essays is a love letter to them and how their love and support got me to this place.

I spend a lot of time thinking about the idea and practice of places. There are the inaccessible places with broken railings and elevators. There are the comfortable and beautiful places that feel like home and possibility. And there are the places that fall somewhere in between, that are neither good nor bad but exist just the same, like the Medium Place on NBC's *The Good Place*. That is the magic of place: it can be anything and everything all at once. I said in a poem once that I often think of my body as a place and not a thing. But my body became a place, a home, only when I started loving it. Before love, my body was a thing, a cage holding me hostage and keeping me when I desperately wanted to be elsewhere. Before love, my body was a thing to pity and hate, a thing for other people to look at and feel grateful wasn't theirs.

The world, in many ways, still sees me and my body this way. Disabled bodies are often used to make the able-bodied feel better about their own bodies; we are a reminder that "it could be worse." I fight anyway for all people to live their best lives, except Nazis, racists, transphobes, homophobes, and the like. I don't care how they feel. I hope they have the worst days and karma does what it has to do when the time comes.

I refuse to be a reminder of someone's worst-case scenario again. If you need me to be a reminder, I will be your reminder that things will get better. I will be a reminder that people like me exist and thrive and that we aren't going anywhere. Long gone are the days of silence and complacency. I will see and be seen, and I no longer care about the comfort of those who would rather I be quiet or wait my turn for proper and positive representation in our culture and mainstream media. Disabled people are at once invisible and a burden. In the rare event that Hollywood decides to depict us, we are seen only as white male wheelchair users who hate themselves. There is nothing inherently wrong about telling the stories of the white and male wheelchair users—their stories are important—but there are also other stories worth telling.

My hope is that this collection will help change the preconceived notion of what disability looks like. My hope is that these stories will encourage you to confront your own biases and ideals while reading about experiences outside of your own. My hope is that you will understand that this collection is a journey of joy and acceptance.

The Pretty One is a collection for the people who give a damn, for the girl who saw her differences as dangerous and ugly, who lived most of her life trying desperately to wish herself into another body, for the person who just wants to experience joy through a little sadness and laughter along the way. *The Pretty One* is for you, the person choosing to read it. I hope you have fun reading my words and laugh at all the appropriate and inappropriate parts that have made my life what it is so far. So turn the page, and let's do this thing!

CAN WE SIT FOR A SEC?

My longest relationship has been with chairs. We are very happy to-gether, committed and strong, in sickness and health till death do us part, etc. There are arguments and disagreements as in any other re-lationship, but we apologize and make up before nightfall so we don't go to bed angry. The notion of love at first sight is a little cheesy but true. Chairs and I have traveled around the world and back again. We cuddled on the beach in Puerto Rico, shared stolen glances in the Virgin Islands, danced the night away in Grand Turk, and gave some major PDA in the Bahamas. My chairs are loyal, with vastly different personalities but an equal amount of appreciation for the butt of mine that sits in them. A few of them like to play it cool: they don't want me to think that they care as much as they do, and I let them believe that it's working. After all, sometimes you have to let your partner think they have the upper hand, to work toward the long game of the bigger thing you want later. However, you and I, dear reader, we know the truth. The chairs in my life love me, and I honestly can't blame them.

My favorite place to canoodle with my boo is at the mall. I love shopping. It brings me the kind of joy that I imagine having a child brings to a mother. Shopping is euphoric for me. It is my personal treat after long days. When shopping, I always feel like anything is possible, like the world is at my fingertips, waiting for me to step out in my new outfits and live my best life. Several times, I have bought a few items I've forgotten to wear and have found them months later with their tags still on.

In new clothes, I feel like I am debuting the best versions of myself to the world. I like to wear them where I know enough people will see me, because if enough people don't see your cute outfit, did you even wear one at all? In these moments, I enjoy the audience I often receive just for existing. In new clothes, I don't care who stares. Strangers are often looking for a show from me, so why not give them one? If I am going to stand out, at least I will look cute while I do it. New clothes are great for all those reasons—as well as for the option of pairing them with beloved older pieces already in my wardrobe, as an excuse to wear those pieces one more time. And, of course, the smell and feel of new clothes is a beautiful thing.

When I am at the mall, I often ask myself, "What can I buy that I certainly don't need?" Ice cream, a cookie, a pretzel? All three. How many items of clothing can I buy without trying them on? I believe my record is four full outfits and a cute pair of shoes. You can never have enough of the thing that brings you comfort.

I love going to the mall with my friends Felicia Kazmierczak, Christine Goings ("Tinni"), Jenny Cerne, and Leigh Rechin. They are fast walkers and know by now that three stores in I'll be wheezing like I ran a mile. They are great friends, always asking if I am all right and if I need to sit down. They even slow down for me, waiting patiently for me to catch up. Still, I refuse to sit, because I love a challenge. I seem to enjoy pushing my body to its limits, feeling unsatisfied until I am using a clothing rack for support while pretending to look at a shirt that is either hideous or too small for me. Sometimes

I sneak to the back of the store, where the shoes are, just to catch my breath out of my friends' line of sight. Despite their unending kindness, I still feel embarrassed when I do this.

When I give in to my body's protests, I find refuge on the benches outside my favorite stores—despite how immensely uncomfortable they are and seem to be proud about it. These benches are not technically chairs, so they don't feel the love for me, they don't care for my comfort, and I try not to take it personally. I also aim to spend not too much time on them, but desperate times call for desperate measures and my aching bones don't care about my strained relationships. I liken these benches to the kids in high school who spend so much time trying to convince everyone that they don't care about anything or anyone—yet in their attempts, it is clear that the opposite is true. I was that teenager and I remember her most in these moments. The malls that I frequent place these benches as if to say, "You can rest for a moment, but we aren't happy about it. We have money to make and no time to waste. Get up and go buy something." So of course, I obey and buy a bunch of things I don't need but really want, and that's basically the same thing, right? We owe ourselves those little pleasures in life.

....

One of the fondest memories I have from college was a night when my friends and I were leaving our galleria mall and heading back to our college town of Fredonia. Now, for context, we had decided to take this trip to the mall in the evening, after classes had finished for the day. So by the time we were done shopping, it was pitch-black outside. The four of us—Felicia, Tinni, Jenny, and I—were singing Backstreet Boys at the top of our lungs. I was belting off-key and with vigor, trying to hit the high note in "All I Have to Give," when we missed our exit. To this day I am unsure if I was the true reason Felicia forgot to make the proper turn, but if I was, it was probably because she was so mesmerized by my clear vocal ability. After realizing our mistake, we learned that we needed gas before we even tried to find our way back to school. In our desperation, we ended up in one of those small towns you see at the beginning of a horror movie. The ones where you see a tumbleweed roll across the screen and a man with a machete at some point, the places that are too quiet and too deserted, with the kind of guy who would ask, "Are you sure you ladies should be out this late?" all with a sinister smile on his face and scary music playing in the background that every person but us can hear. I had had this experience only once before, with Leigh at her cottage: I had forgotten to bring my toothbrush, so we stopped at a gas station and I sat in her car but made her go in for me because it looked like the gas station where Q from *One Tree Hill* was shot. I couldn't take any chances.

There is a truth universally acknowledged that in the horror genre (with the exception of the critically acclaimed *Get Out*), black people are usually the first to die. This truth is evident in *Spider Baby*, in which Mantan Moreland is killed in the first few minutes, and in *Scream 2*, in which Jada Pinkett Smith and Omar Epps are killed in the first few minutes. As I was the only black person in the car, and with the creepy town ahead of us, my chances of survival were looking slim. My only solace was the fact that Felicia's car seats were much more comfortable than the benches outside the stores; if I died, at least I'd know both my butt and right leg were satisfied.

I did have a laugh when I decided to share this information with my friends, most of whom rolled their eyes and laughed—except for Jenny, who looked at me and said, "No, don't say that. You are going to be fine." This was funny especially because Jenny is the nicest person in the world. She takes you at your word, and that is why I believe a part of her thought I was serious and not being the casual dramatic that I can be. In the end, I didn't die first or last in that creepy abandoned town, but having narrowly escaped a horror movie death for the second time in my life, I did remember feeling that those girls would be my friends for the rest of my life. (As Tinni and I sat in folding chairs at Felicia's wedding party table on August 5, 2017, I knew that my gut feeling from that night had been exactly right.)

If you don't need to rest with the help of chairs the way I do, you're lucky, not in the sense that those who do are unlucky, but because the ability to navigate the world without giving a second thought to accommodations must be very nice. In the event that you do, welcome to the club, friend. I know how exhausting life can be, but maybe someday we will sit next to each other in the comfortable and soft chairs we deserve.

During our freshman year of college, my friends and I spent ample amounts of time at house parties chair-dancing in old recliners and stained couches, swaying to songs that were much too fast, and giggling uncontrollably the way you do when you're tipsy and have the energy to stay out all night. When we stayed in, we did so to play card games like Threethirteen and Poophead. We played on the floors of our dorm rooms and in the empty common room, sitting in the tall wooden chairs for hours listening to Pandora until we were too tired to keep our eyes open. I miss those tables and chairs as much as I miss my friends. They were not particularly comfortable or exciting, but they were a part of my college experience, the nights when I knew that I had been chosen by the right people, people who were okay with Dragon Berry rum and ginger ale in plastic cups and laughing until I cried and almost fell out of those chairs. People who sat with me while I rested my bones and allowed me to pretend that I was not beat and a little bruised. People who sit with me still.

....

When I am not with my friends at the mall taking short breaks to visit my unrequited bench love while he sits bored and feeling inconvenienced, or when I'm not missing exits over sing-alongs or traveling abroad with my boo, we stay in. The chair I am most committed to is actually a deep brown couch in my living room, where I do almost everything, from TV watching to writing about TV and talking to the people who star in the shows. I have written much of this book on that couch. I often choose to sit on the far left of the couch because it has been kind to me as the comfiest part of the chair. In reality, I am sure that it is just the section that has gotten used to the shape of my butt—by force, not enjoyment—but she never complains, either way.

Now, this couch, let's call her Vivian. (Trust me, she looks like a Vivian.) Vivian isn't into PDA. She keeps to herself, very quiet and demure but confident. She gets me in a way that the bench from the mall does not. She cares about my comfort and well-being, and she doesn't push me to spend money I don't have. I love her in the way you do a well-worn partner with whom you have weathered many a storm. Though she isn't as old as she seems. She expects more of me the way the people closest to you do, because they know your potential.

Vivian is stern but caring. She knows her worth and purpose and understands when to make herself uncomfortable in order to make me move. She has my best interests at heart and provides the kind of comfortable and easy relief that you might take for granted, convinced that it will always be there no matter what. We can sit in silence without the urgency to fill the space with words, the way one can when one is not trying to impress the other thing or person in the room. Together we have seen many rejections and acceptances, as many good times and badly aching bones as you'd imagine, as well as the in-between, the not-good-but-not-bad days. The days when I can't be productive enough to write at my computer but can brainstorm in the Notes app on my phone. She doesn't make me feel like I have to apologize even when I do. I will love Vivian long after she is gone or long after I am living under the California sun with new couches and chairs to fall in love with. Vivian is the best of seats. Don't tell the others.

Sometimes, when I can get away, I have a lover's tryst with a seat we can call Paul. Paul is your everyday movie theater seat. He's comfortable and likes to cuddle and be the big spoon. I imagine he'd wear flannel and chop wood if he could, maybe light the fire for our fireplace if we had one (and he were a human person) or make me coffee with one cream and four sugars, just the way I like it, while the night stretches on but we are not yet tired. He is adventurous but prefers the indoors. We have a lot in common. He loves films as much as I do and hates bugs. He understands that I can never recline my seat too far, otherwise I will fall asleep—and no one wants to fall asleep on a date. We speak quietly and quickly about one day watching a movie that I have written, because we believe in the possibility of that happening. While we are busy believing, the last preview ends and the opening to the film begins. We are never together long enough, only a couple of hours maximum, but when we are together it is magical.

The true magic of our relationship is the ability to enter new worlds together. Paul and I don't get to see each other often, because movies are expensive and he can never get away from work, but when I sit in him, he takes away all my worries, eases my hip pain, and allows my imagination to run wild. He is so supportive of my dreams and reminds me to always work toward them even when they feel impossible, especially the big ones. We have watched so many great movies together and a few very bad ones, but we always have great stories to tell later, regardless. Paul is patient. He has to be, for the way he is treated by other moviegoers. I made him a promise early on that I would never treat him the same way some do when they leave messes in his home. This promise may be the very reason that whenever we see each other, I always have the best view of our date-night movie.

Outside of malls, home couches, and movie theaters, I tell my own stories to crowds of strangers, some of whom have become my friends. I have sat on studio set couches for morning shows like *AM Buffalo*, chairs atop stages like the ones in Portland at the Affect Conf and at the Albright-Knox Art Gallery in Buffalo, New York, for the Radical Women's Night Out panel. I have sat in a comfortable but oddly shaped chair during a disability and ethics symposium keynote speech at DePauw University. My words have allowed me the opportunity to travel to places I have never been to, and to get to those places, I have to sit in a certain seat—let's call him Brandon. Brandon is your standard small and uncomfortable airline seat. He's got a bit of an attitude problem, but it is an understandable one. He is already bored of you before you meet and would happily relay your most embarrassing secrets that you told him in confidence if he could.

The seats in coach are named Brandon, not those in first class. I have never been in the first-class seats, but I've named them Oscar after Oscar Isaac because he is dreamy and they are the dream. Anyway, Brandon is small and uncomfortable and bearable only once you think of being elsewhere the entire time you are together. (Elsewhere like your planned destination.) Brandon doesn't believe in personal space; he can't, since I sit atop him, and someone else, often a stranger, sits right next to me on his brother. Still, Brandon has taken me to new places, so I cannot be too hard on him.

The most difficult boyfriend seats, though, are those in waiting rooms. They aren't comfortable and they aren't supposed to be, no matter how long you are made to wait. As a trusted source who has spent most of her life in and out of doctors' offices—from the waiting rooms for specialists to hospitals before surgeries and follow-ups for post-ops—I can tell you that these chairs are necessary yet terrible, and not simply due to their exposed stuffing or dull colors. There is the anxiety, too. Hospitals in particular make me anxious; they always have. Every surgery I have ever had was necessary, every operating room table I sat on before lying down was sturdy enough to do what it was supposed to do. I have been very lucky in that I have experienced no complications or problems during surgery, but my anxiety does not care for facts or reason. Sitting in those waiting rooms for follow-ups through weeks and months always left me petrified that something had gone wrong and I would have to go back under the knife.

The loss of control is where the true manifestation of my anxiety begins: the fact that you're put under and you have no idea what is being done to your body, but you lead with the hope that it is the right thing, as strangers cut into your body in an effort to make it better. The reality is that I frequently cut myself open in the figurative sense when I share bits of myself with readers and audiences, but the idea of being cut open in real life will never not worry me despite the many experiences I have had. My fear is doubled when a loved one is in the position of appointments or surgeries, as my loved one and I wait for test results or to get blood work done. The act of waiting to know whether everything is going to be okay or not is the hardest part, and no chair could make it easier. Yet at the same time, despite my fear of these chairs, they do provide a semblance of rest for my body, and that is what is most important.

The chairs I am most excited for are the ones I hope to sit in at bookstores across the country one day. As a firm believer in dreaming big, I dream of monumental chairs for monumental moments. Right now, I dream of tall, dark wood chairs, like the ones on HGTV that demand attention in every room. As a lover of dark wood furniture, I envision it in a lot of my professional fantasies: the dream home office with the deep, dark hardwood floors and chairs to match, with a lot of natural sunlight shining on everything. You can't sit in these types of wooden chairs for long, but at the time, it is worth it.

The excitement of grand chairs in a bookstore sustains me. I like to picture myself behind a white table sitting in a chair with enough cushion to keep me from having to shift my weight, a pen in my hand, ready and waiting to be used. Nothing would be better than reading my words to a willing audience, telling stories that matter to me and to someone else in or outside my lived experiences. To be able to sit and rest my bones while doing so? A win-win.

....

I guess this is the point where I tell you why I love or fear so many chairs and need to sit in them. I'm not lazy or tired, though sometimes my exhaustion makes the need to sit in those chairs necessary. I don't give chairs names and personality traits out of obligation. I do it because I find humor and fun in it. In reality, who doesn't need the mall benches or the comfort of a friend's car from time to time? We all sit in movie theater seats and dream of life-affirming travel. But the reason I have to often sit and rest is because of my cerebral palsy.

My cerebral palsy is the annoying but endearing best friend in your favorite romantic comedy: the friend who doesn't end up with the love interest but who seems happy with her life as it is (so you don't necessarily feel like justice wasn't done by the time the credits roll). The friend who causes you quite a bit of strife, but you can complain because she's your friend. (If others tried to, you'd shut them down, even if they were a little right, because at the end of the day it's all about loyalty, and you should at least be loyal to yourself and your people.) Cerebral palsy doesn't always return the favor, though. Our love is a little one-sided. A thing she likes to do is make my body ache at the most inconvenient times, like when I'm shopping or on vacation or at the movies. We both end up losing. Sometimes, if I'm unlucky, she will tap the pain into the fight while I'm already sitting down and not doing anything extraneous. I think she does it so that she can keep me on my toes, but I think it's a bit much. Secretly, I think she likes being the center of attention; after all, in all these places, she makes people stare. Often people stare at us so hard they run into things and could catch flies with how wide their mouths hang open. That part is funny once you get past the initial agitation. They behave as though they've never seen someone limp before, as though there is magic in my scarred and bent fingertips.

When I sat in a rolling desk chair at a summer park office job just before I started college, I felt like a real adult, one who would tell the visiting children that those fingers were magic, could grant three wishes if they believed hard enough. I told them this because I was ashamed at the truth, which was that I thought there was nothing beautiful about them. But I found solace when I was able to sit back down in my rolling desk chair once more. Rolling desks chairs are fun for the obvious reasons—I have never met a person who didn't love to spin in them—but those chairs also never cared how I looked, didn't watch my confusion about how to navigate a room. They never asked questions, just kept me up and able to do my work, to answer phones in an effort to prove my competence and pretend I wasn't bothered by the questions the children asked me. Despite my love for her, I was so embarrassed of my rolling desk chair back then, like the teenager of a parent who tries too hard to be cool when dropping his kid off at school.

That job and the chair are long gone, replaced by the black couch of my former boss at the park, Melissa Junke, who is now a close friend. In her home, along with my sister, Leah, and her best friend, Kandyce, we reminisce about those summers. How we survived them and grew as people because of them—and because we have each other. In her home, sitting on her black couch or in the chairs on her back patio with music blaring under the summer sun and laughter pooling out of us from the tips of our toes to the roofs of our mouths, I don't care how I look, and I do not have to. I also don't have to answer any disability questions, because my friends are not curious enough to care; they have known me all my life, and that's the beauty of lifelong relationships: they know everything they need to know and things they probably wish that they didn't. I don't have to wear a brave face or perform happiness or indifference with them. All that I have to do is be myself. "Club 41," we affectionately call her home (41 is her house number; the name came after a random night when we were laughing and dancing before declaring that we felt like we were out at a club without the effort). There, I am surrounded by the comfort that the office chair once gave me: along with great food, even better people, and enough laughter to make my stomach hurt in the best way.

....

For every bit of frustration, self-consciousness, and agitation that my cerebral palsy brings me, for every moment that I am tired and out of breath, I remember that this cerebral palsy is mine. We know each other like the back of our hands, and even when I catch myself wishing for the relief that would come in a body without CP, I stop and think of all the great people this body has given me the opportunity to know and all the great chairs that I have been able to sit in. When I went back to speak at my alma mater in April 2017, as part of a four-years-out program where grads speak to students in their same degree about life after college and what it takes to succeed, I sat in a variety of chairs. I sat in strangely shaped but aesthetically pleasing ones and clear chairs that swiveled in the school's science building, where I did a small photo shoot for a separate profile. I sat in a lot of folding chairs as I answered questions and reassured students that the work would not be easy but would matter as long as it mattered to them. I sat on bar stools and wooden chairs as those same kids bought me and my friend and fellow speaker Kelley drinks as a thank-you that night. By the end of the weekend, I thought back on my own graduation in 2013, when I sat in a black folding chair too excited to be uncomfortable and smiling from ear to ear with the knowledge that every single part of me had helped in getting me to that moment, even if I couldn't quite appreciate every part of me at that time.

I didn't appreciate almost any part of me growing up, but I appreciated every chair for providing my young body with solace. Growing up, I hated nothing more than when a friend or loved one said to me, "If you didn't have CP, you wouldn't be you." I hated it in part because I didn't want to be me with cerebral palsy. I was tired of being tired and having to rest while playing at the park with my sister and cousins, having to take breaks and sit on benches inside the shelter while the other kids ran around without a care in the world. It was infuriating and embarrassing to be so young and to need so many breaks. That kind of thinking is entrenched in the "youth is health" ideology, but I would not learn that until later. I felt cursed, but not in the fun, campy, *Hocus Pocus* way. I didn't want to be me with cerebral palsy when I'd walk into my grandmother's house winded from a day of playing outside, or into a college classroom feeling breathless, a resulting pain shooting through me long before I reached the security of the uncomfortable desks. I thought of people telling me I "wouldn't be me" in these moments and scoffed. What did anyone else really know about my pain?

Now, at twenty-seven, as I sit in Vivian surrounded by her comfort and familiarity, or as I sit in any chair I come across in the world, I feel as though I finally understand what was being said to me. My life might be a lot easier physically without cerebral palsy. I can't say that I would miss the limited range of motion and the aching bones, but I'd miss the bond with the inanimate object of my heart that I choose to give life to, the way it gives to me: chairs. This me, the one with CP, is the only me I've ever known. She is hard to live with sometimes, because pain can fog up all the love you think you feel, all the things you think you learned. When I am in pain I don't care about cutting her slack or sugarcoating the ways I hurt her, because she is hurting me back and I fear I deserve it. In the end, though, she knows my heart.

....

We are getting a bit off track, though. This essay is about my first true love, chairs, and the way they often hold me together physically, calming me through heavy breaths desperate for equilibrium and providing relief while I take care of the mental work. The key to living fully and as well as possible is comfort, after all, and I'm grateful for the chairs and seats that provide me not only with comfort and joy but also relief from what would otherwise be unbearable pain. That's the truth of disability I was once so scared to admit was an aspect of my experience: the pain. Living in a culture that is eager to view pain under the arc of motivation or as a tool to lean in to because it will ultimately lead us to surpass whatever obstacle is in our way gives me pause in my explanation of my own pain. I try not to talk about the days when I can't believe that my body wants what is best for me as I lie and then sit on my bed with packs of ice and a heating pad—but I *should*, because they are a part of me as much as the cheesy tweets, the essays and articles, the good days.

Sometimes my beloved chairs are not enough to heal me and I have to pull out of things that I would have loved to participate in otherwise. Chairs are not as healing as they should be, and that is where modern medicine comes in. There was the time when I could not go to my friend's birthday dinner two years in a row because on each night my hip was screaming in pain. There are the times when I've had to bow out of local festivals because of the strain walking long distances would put on my legs. There was the time when I missed a full day of activities at a conference because I was both sick and in pain, and the time I had to stay back during the night-out portion of my friends' bachelorette party because I was in so much pain I was crying at the restaurant. I cursed chairs for not being enough to get me up and moving.

When chairs are enough, though—and they often are—joy is always right around the corner due to their replenishing powers. Joy is waiting to be noticed by my relieved eyes. Whether that joy comes in the form of watching two of my best friends get married, missing exits after nineties-music sing-alongs, having lunch dates on Vivian with my aunt Regina, graduating from college, and going viral and being interviewed by major publications, it is joy that keeps me moving forward. My joy is possible in part only because in the midst of it the chairs are there, waiting patiently for me should I need them. The relief is contingent on both the joy and pain because it comes when my body hurts so intently that the most I can do is lie back and prop up my leg and remind myself that even on my worst days, my cerebral palsy has gotten me this far, so she must not be that bad. Relief comes when I narrowly escape the pain I was so sure was inevitable. I wouldn't be the me I know (and finally like) without the CP, and maybe that means it is worth something, even with the way it can make my body ache and throb.

If there is anything CP has given me that is good, it is the opportunity to meet and fall in love with new chairs and new seats, to get to know them on first sit-dates as we discover what level of comfort will be offered to my body and how long the comfort will last. You should get to know who or what you are spending hours sitting atop out of courtesy. We get to know each other, the things we like, what we don't, and because all great relationships have boundaries, we do, too. For the long-term chairs in my life, we establish ground rules very quickly. We have to, because when it feels right you just know and do not have the time to waste. For the temporary chairs it is like speed dating. Will we be fine together for a day? A night? A moment? We are not looking for commitment, just temporary comfort on my part, and to be used on theirs. There is still work I must do alone. I work not to use my chairs as crutches so that I remain inactive and antisocial when my anxiety manifests itself as phantom pain. The good news is that I can do my work while they do theirs. They work to provide me with moments of rejuvenation both big and small. Once we are past the first sit-date and the defining of the relationship, we enter the lovey-dovey phase. Here we are a well-oiled machine, a weather-worn and tested love of the ages.

In this phase of our relationship, I spend as much time as possible in my chosen chair despite every request I get to leave it and be social. We are inseparable, excited to watch TV, write, interview, and relax together. The love is new and therefore I see no fault in the chair that I have chosen, ignoring red flags like their color, thin cushioning, or rickety legs. We can't both be barely holding it together, but sometimes that's how it happens. In this phase, I am always trying to look my best whenever I occupy its space, trick it into believing this is what it will always get from me even though we both know the truth. I also find myself being uncharacteristically careful with what and how I eat while in the chair. I am careful not to spill on it and damage what we are building together. It is very easy to see why I am single in these moments, because I am genuinely concerned about how the chairs will perceive me. We will eventually fall out of the infatuation phase but remain close enough to reach an understanding that we want the same thing: to be meaningful to each other's lives.

....

The truth is, chairs are a meaningful part of my life and the lives of disabled folks alike who need a moment, a place to just be as the world moves around us at whatever pace it chooses. Chairs are a functioning reprieve from the harsh realities of the world, and they often give us tickets to see it in all of its beauty and problems, because no one place is perfect—but it is nice to be in places that come close.

As I've already made clear, I love chairs, and I wrote this essay not just because I was trying to be funny (though I hope you laughed a bit) but also because all too often we equate sitting and resting, taking breaks and catching our breath, with inherent laziness. There is a belief that we must always keep moving and pushing ourselves well beyond our limits to please others or their ideas of who we are supposed to be. This is a philosophy that has proved to be harmful for many people. I sometimes buy into the idea against my better judgment, too. I push my body to its limits and beyond because I try to be the person who strangers expect, the disabled girl who is beating the odds, despite my knowing how ridiculous that notion is. I recognize the fact that I sometimes don't practice what I preach, but that's why, for me, chairs are not just punch lines to an essay or a joke but the objects that keep me able to rest up and in turn be active in my body. While I continue to acknowledge that rest can also keep me healthier and energized enough to be lively in the long run, this also means that I have to acknowledge that no disabled person should have to be active or constantly moving to push themselves past unhealthy limits to be valued. There is no right or wrong way or reason to rest in your chairs when your body is telling you to slow down.

Chairs are amazing and don't get the credit that they deserve. Have you thanked a chair today? Maybe hug the next one you see and remember that they are there for a reason and they are helping people in small and big ways. They keep the people you love able to participate in your lives in a way that they might not be able to otherwise.

It is kind of a funny thing to think about, isn't it? A chair having such an impact on someone's life. Well, I implore you to think of your life without them. What would your world look like? Sure, eating standing up would be okay at first, but the sheen would wear off really fast. Driving without chairs in your car is not only illegal but downright dangerous. It is hard to imagine schools without desks, which are an integral part of the classroom. Sure, there are offices without swivel chairs, but I am certain they could not function without any chairs at all. If you left work and came home to a kitchen table without chairs, would it not surprise you? Whether you eat with your family around the table talking about your days or you eat alone with your pet without chairs, the sitting would be a little harder, especially if your knees aren't what they used to be. The specific intimacy that a simple thing like chairs can create would cease to exist.

We have to rid ourselves of the idea that health means constant movement and that stillness is laziness. In the reality of most people's bodies, constant movement may mean muscle strain and excessive pain, which can lead to even bigger problems with our physical health. Being active is important, but the belief that a certain level of excessive activity can keep anyone healthy is misguided at best. If it were true, then how can we explain the people with "perfect health" who have blood clots that lead to heart attacks and strokes? Our bodies are not as cut-and-dry or black-and-white as we would like to believe them to be, and neither are human beings. That's what makes the world so fascinating.

Our culture scoffs at people who use the elevator, especially those of us whose disabilities might be invisible, and it invents things like the Vycle, a stationary-like bike that forces you to pedal in order to get to another floor in place of an elevator. The idea seems cool and exciting at first until you remember what I've told you. We live in a world that designs things under the assumption that everybody in the world is able-bodied and fully functioning at all times. The assumption that elevators are used only as a vehicle for laziness is ableist. The Vycle promises to use less energy than the standard elevator, but whose energy is really being saved here? Not the energy of disabled folks who do not have the leg strength to pedal a bike just to get to a floor in a building they occupy. Now, I am not here to crap on someone else's creative invention; as a creator, I get it. My goal is to challenge the inherent thoughts and ideas we have when we think of the "environmentally friendly and energy-saving" things we create. Ableism, whether it is intentional or not, is at the root of many of these inventions, and it leads people to believe that they know what's best for the bodies of everyone when their products really cater only to a small subset of people with bodies like those of the creators themselves.

When we remember that no one body is the same as another and acknowledge the privilege behind our aversions to the necessity of objects like chairs and stools as tools to allow others to exist in spaces that they could not exist in otherwise, we will be in a better place as a society. Essentially, seeking out experiences that do not reflect our own and trying to understand the complexities of our bodies and the tools we have to navigate with will make room for real change and growth, as well as for innovation that can give us all the quality of life that we deserve outside of the toxic need to earn what should already be a right; specifically, a moment of rest. My greatest worry is losing people in this world simply because they overexerted themselves trying to keep up at work, home, sports, or the like. It is our responsibility to take some of the cultural pressure off.

My hope is that someday proper accessibility won't be so hard to come by and essays like these can be all jokes. Until then, you'll have this one to hold you over. Why do we push ourselves past our limits? Not the limits that make us better in the long run, but the limits that harm our body? And why do we police the bodies and needs of others? My guess is that we do it to feel better about our own. Insecurity is often the catalyst that sparks most judgments. Once we rid ourselves of our judgment of others and of ourselves, we can be honest about why we take such issue with the health and well-being of others outside the thin and able-bodied category. I think that when we do this, we will realize what a waste of time judging others harshly has been, because we strive toward an ideal body and health that isn't even possible or attainable for the people in the bodies we are supposed to be envying and working to achieve. So cut yourself some slack, pull up a chair, and hang out for a while. The world will not stop if you give your body the rest I am certain it deserves. My longest relationship has been with chairs, and we're very happy together. I am forever grateful for all that they have given me and all that they will.

LOVE YOU, MEAN IT

Jealousy is a funny thing. We often laugh at the jealousy portrayed in popular culture, or cringe because we see ourselves and our own jealousy reflected in it. One of my favorite representations of overt jealousy is in the film *The Wedding Date*. I can quote this movie almost front to back. I've seen it more times than I can count. If you are unfamiliar, *The Wedding Date* tells the story of Kat (Debra Messing), a single woman preparing to attend the wedding of her younger sister, Amy (Amy Adams). *The Wedding Date* is one of my favorite movies because I love the chemistry between the two main characters, I love a romantic comedy with wit, and I love Debra Messing. However, it wasn't until recently that, contrary to the perceived understanding that Kat is jealous of Amy because there has always been an unspoken competition between them, I realized just how jealous Amy actually was of Kat. There is pressure on them both, but the brunt of familial disappointment is placed on Kat, by her mother especially. Kat is seen as the sister whose fiancé dumped her out of the blue, leaving her family with the wedding costs and herself without love, all the while being reminded that she "should" have been the first to marry because she is the oldest sister.

Kat's younger half sister, Amy, seems like she has it all. She's younger than Kat, which is a huge point of contention, and she marries the man of her dreams, with Kat's ex as the best man. Meanwhile, Kat hires an escort so she won't have to face the weekend and her family's concerned faces alone. Kat is a ball of nerves as she meets Nick, the escort (played by Dermot Mulroney), on the plane for the first time right before they take off. Once they land in London, where Kat's family is, they head to a rehearsal dinner, where Kat and Amy's mother drunkenly muses that they all thought Kat would marry before Amy and how the family couldn't get the deposit back from her wedding venue. Kat is mortified, while Amy laughs awkwardly but seems to move on quickly, worried less about how Kat feels and more about how the outburst looks at the party that's supposed to be about her.

Amy's jealousy manifests itself in quick and slick comments to Kat, as well as in the expectation that the world should bend to her will. At the engagement party, Amy expects Kat to give her the drink Kat ordered for herself because Amy's is taking too long. At the bachelorette party, Amy drunkenly rattles off that Kat is an expat who had all the boys' attention when they were growing up, neglecting to mention the fact that Amy slept with Kat's ex repeatedly while he and Kat were together—and that it happened again when Kat's ex, Jeffrey (Jeremy Sheffield), ended their engagement because he fell in love with Amy after Kat moved away. Amy does these things because of her own insecurities and the desire to have what Kat once had. Amy's jealousy gives way to selfishness. Her guilt about ending up with Jeffrey is what keeps her from telling Kat the truth until years later.

Although I feel that Kat forgives Amy too quickly in the movie, I understand the insecurities that lead Amy to the decisions she makes. I would never do the same things to my twin sister, Leah, but for a long time I wanted what Leah had in terms of her physical appearance. I was insecure in regard to my relationship with her and in my own comparisons to her.

Jealousy is a thing that no one really likes to talk about, because it forces us to confront the harshest parts of our instinctive insecurities. We'd all like to believe that we have evolved past jealousy, but even the most successful and gorgeous people are jealous of someone else. I think our discomfort around jealousy comes from the fact that even though we know that it serves no positive purpose in our lives, we still find ourselves succumbing to the temptation of it. I believe that being uncomfortable is important in order for us to grow.

I am not sitting on a high horse and writing about jealousy as an abstract thing. In fact, at one point in my life I was more jealous of my twin sister than I was of anyone else in the world—and I relished this. Jealousy was easy. It felt like the best and worst thing every time it found its way into moments I shared with Leah. Jealousy was the first to arrive and the last to leave most interactions we had with each other. I might not have been getting married to the man of my dreams when I confronted my jealousy for the first time, but I made the same kind of slick comments about how, like Kat, Leah was the one who had the attention of boys and men, as though it were a personal slight against me. I also made the choice to remain selfish in the same way that Amy is with respect to Kat for most of the movie. I was determined to hurt Leah the way I had convinced myself she had hurt me, by her simply being better than me. When I asked for her forgiveness, as Amy asks Kat for hers, I didn't expect her to forgive me, in the same way that Amy does not expect Kat to forgive her, but I was grateful for Leah's forgiveness, and, as in *The Wedding*

Date, the act of forgiveness proved that I had a lot of growing up to do. Furthermore, a lot of necessary introspection took place on my part as a result.

Leah and I aren't like the twins you see on your TV screens. We don't finish each other's sentences or confuse people by switching places. We also don't appear out of thin air together in an effort to creep people out, like the twins from *The Shining*. We are identical twins but hear more often than not that we don't really look alike. I don't know if my cerebral palsy is a factor in our vast differences, but I think when the lights and angles are right, we do look a lot more alike than people think. At least, that is what my mother says. On occasion we do say the same thing at the same time, which always makes us laugh, but that's rare. Regardless, Leah is my twin sister and wombmate, even if other people don't see the resemblance. We were raised in the way twins often are, with matching clothes in different colors. I was a bald-headed baby who cried a lot and was often mistaken for a boy, even in my all-pink outfits. Leah was quiet, had hair, and didn't mind having her picture taken. We were premature babies born in September when we were supposed to have been born in January. Weighing in at one pound, six ounces, and one pound, nine ounces—Leah and me, respectively—we spent the first three months of our lives in the neonatal intensive care unit.

In the cheesiest and most literal sense, I have never known the world without Leah, and I don't ever want to. If I move across the country to Los Angeles at some point, I see myself FaceTiming her just to tell her that I'm not doing anything, or calling her to ask about the lyrics of a song we sang as kids—anything, really, to make sure we don't lose the knowledge that we are in the world at the same time and there is a magic to that. We live in the same city and in the same house right now, though, so instead I make a lot of jokes on our birthday each year about Leah needing to respect her elder because I am a minute older than she is (it counts, I promise). The numbers matter, because there are now four sets of twins in my family: my cousins Mykele and Melaine are three years younger than Leah and me, and we have another set of twin cousins, and then one set from my cousin Mahogony Allen and the other from my cousin Jasmine Whitt. I like to think that Leah and I led the pack.

My very first memories are of Leah right beside me, whether walking into preschool, stealing her line in the play when she was too shy to say it, or arguing over whose shoe was whose. Leah and I were a package deal. If you heard my name, Leah's was sure to follow, and when family members wanted one of us to do something but didn't care which one, they affectionately referred to us as "the twins." They would say, "One of the twins, come help me with [this or that thing]," or, "One of you close the door," or "turn on that light." We were one and the same, and even as an adult black woman who loves her individuality now, I loved that unity when I was growing up.

I was raised never knowing that my body was different and that I was the other in our family. I played in parks, rode scooters up and down the sidewalk at my grandmother's house, rolled around grass hills at cheerleading practice, and step-ball-changed in dance class right alongside Leah. We didn't like to sit still for long. We were always busy and always on the go. The world had too much to offer to slow us down or make us pause in fear or worry about what people saw when they looked at us. In many ways, that is what I miss most about my childhood, the way in which I lived my life without caring what others thought when they looked at me.

When Leah and I weren't dancing, cheering, playing, and being everyday active kids, we spent our time watching all the Mary-Kate and Ashley Olsen movies we owned. We could recite the movies line by line; we could even recite the advertisement for their dolls that came on right before the movies began. We loved Mary-Kate and Ashley so much, though I think I loved them more. I wanted Leah and me to be their best friends. I wanted them to know we existed in the world. In my head, I'd refer to us as "the black Mary-Kate and Ashley." When we watched their movies, I longed to experience the same things they did; the trips to London, Salt Lake City, Rome, and Paris; and the experiences with boys. The strange thing is that even when I was old enough to know that a movie was made just for entertainment purposes and not something that was happening in real time, I still felt like Leah and I were getting glimpses into what Mary-Kate and Ashley's life and relationship with each other were really like.

Growing up, we were also big fans of Tia and Tamera Mowry and *Sister, Sister*. Their black skin made me feel close to them. Leah and I watched every episode from the pilot to the finale as Tia and Tamera dealt with everything from trying to learn more about their birth parents to cigarettes, individuality, and fashion, and I envied their bond as much as I envied Mary-Kate and Ashley's. The telling thing about this envy was that even as a child I knew that Leah and I would never have that bond, whether it was because some twins never did or because, deep down, I knew I would grow up resentful that I did not look enough like Leah. I wanted the closeness I perceived other twins had, I wanted their ability to say what they were thinking to each other with a simple look, but I robbed Leah and myself of that relationship before we could ever form it.

When I wasn't idolizing the lives, movies, and shows of celebrity twins, my childhood was spent happily. I was never treated like a burden by my mother, Cheryl, or by my aunts, uncles, cousins, brother, or sister. (I wouldn't feel like one until much later.) My childhood was spent running and playing with my able-bodied family members, leaving only guaranteed grass stains and mud on my clothing. My mother was keen on giving me every Rollerblade, bike, and scooter that my brother and sister had. She never wanted me to feel like I couldn't do what my siblings could do with a little bit of practice, determination, and a few modifications. We didn't talk about my disability that often growing up—which, as I get older, I realize was both great and bad. The not-talking-about-disability as a defining part of who I was was great because I saw myself as just another kid who was as "normal" as the other kids in my house and the friends I made at school, because they never brought up the ways in which I was different from them. I just assumed I mirrored their movement when I walked and talked. Someone was always there to help me if I needed it, so I never took note of my own limitations. I thought I looked like everyone else, because no one ever made me feel like I was a bit different. I do think, though, that a frank conversation about the issues that my disability could bring up in the future or just an understanding that cerebral palsy didn't make me less than my peers or ugly may have allowed me to get to the place I am today a little sooner. I wish I could've saved myself the shock of it all when I discovered the truth.

Our lack of conversation around my disability led me to believe it wasn't a factor in my life. I didn't even know I had a disability until middle school. So, those years from birth to about fifth grade were bliss. When you have no idea that the world is a place that may judge you because of a thing you can't change, it is jarring when you realize that not only is it a possibility but it's a certainty. I was a lucky child for a while, though, in those blissful years, a child who didn't know shame but knew courage and bravery before I knew that my disability would become a stepping-stone to inspiration porn. I never noticed anyone staring or laughing at me, and if I did, I assumed it was for some other reason entirely, such as food caught in my teeth, tissue stuck to my shoe, or a stain visible on my clothes. Still, I can pinpoint the moments when I learned to hate my body and the moment I learned to hate Leah's.

....

There was a kid named Jackson who single-handedly revealed my disability and differences to me when he decided it would be fun to follow me around the lunchroom mimicking my limp. My friends noticed and told him off after alerting me to what he was doing. I laughed like it didn't matter and made my way to a bathroom, where I watched myself in the mirror. As I walked toward it, that's when I knew. I knew that my body was one that was different enough to be made fun of, different enough to warrant ridicule. I cried while walking home from school that day. I begged my mom to tell me why I was like this, why I was the one God had to punish and create different from everyone else. In many ways, this moment in my life jump-started years of self-hatred, disordered eating, and suicidal ideation. Jackson was not the sole reason all this occurred in my life, but he was the beginning. He planted the first seeds of doubt in my worth. The things we do even in jest and naïveté matter; they can change lives. I'm sure that Jackson is probably a nice man and that the decisions of his younger self don't reflect the person that he is today. He probably doesn't remember me or the incident, but it is one that I will never forget.

I know now that disability is not a punishment but a part of who I am, just like the color of my hair or the chubbiness of my cheeks. My disability is both beautiful and aggravating. We have our best and worst days. Sometimes it causes me so much physical pain that I wish I could just will it away, but that isn't how disability works. But young Keah did not know that at the time, and she was angry. That anger at God turned itself into anger at Leah. How dare she walk around beautiful and "normal," with her standard and "normal" working legs and arms, while I walked around like a "freak"? And the older Leah and I got, the deeper my anger took root and grew. I'd pick fights with Leah, call her names, scratch her body by using my stronger left arm, and bite down before she could block me. I did this in a desperate attempt to make her as ugly as I thought I was. I became very desperate around the time boys started to find her attractive and asked me to put in a good word with her. I believed that the attention she received made me uglier.

....

Once in our high school hallway, I had on what I thought was the cutest pair of jeans and a long-sleeved tan shirt from Hollister. I believed that buying cute-enough clothes might ease the strikes against me that came with having a visible disability. I propped myself against some lockers and chatted with my friends before the bell rang for homeroom. While we were talking, they noticed a boy staring intently at me. I don't remember his name or face, but I remember what happened next. I sent a smile his way as he walked toward me, and my friends scurried away in a fit of laughter when he reached my locker. He paused to take a breath before speaking.

"Hey, Keah. How are you?" He shifted his weight from one foot to the other, seemingly nervous.

"I'm great. How about you?" I invoked the flirting tactics I had seen Mary-Kate and Ashley use years earlier. I smiled again and tucked an invisible piece of hair behind my ear.

"Good, good. So, uhhhh . . ." He paused as I was feeling triumphant in what I thought was my ability to make him nervous. He was going to ask me out on my very first date. I was ready, even if I had to laugh at a few unfunny jokes. *Mary-Kate and Ashley, don't let me down.*

"Yes?" I asked again.

"Is Leah seeing anyone? She's really pretty," he stammered. Oh, oh—so the person he was trying to ask out wasn't me but my sister. From what I remember, I wasn't even particularly interested in this boy, just interested in the idea that I was someone worthy of a date. He wasn't the first or the last of the boys to ask me about Leah, so I swallowed my sadness at the rejection and responded.

"She isn't. And before you ask, I'll tell her about you, but I can't guarantee anything."

"Thanks, Keah! You're the best."

I never told Leah about any of the boys who approached me about her. I left all of those good words unsaid because I was angry that they weren't being said about me. I brushed off that rejection and the next and promised never to get my hopes up in regard to boys again . . . until I did. There was another boy who was nice to me when he wanted to be, so naturally, I fell in what I thought was love with him. He did not return those feelings, however, and I spent years afterward on a silent quest to prove to him that I was lovable by someone in the world, somewhere.

To her credit, Leah didn't date a lot in high school, not because she wanted to spare my feelings but because she simply didn't want to. I was always more concerned with all the boys who didn't like me and the girls who might have made fun of me. I often took Leah's lack of concern or care about boys as a personal attack. I didn't understand why she wasn't constantly dating or using her "perfect" able-bodied body the way that I would have. Leah was single because she wanted to be, while I felt I had no other choice. This lack of choice made me angry. Why wouldn't someone take one for the team and date me? Why was Leah the one who had gotten all the good looks? I asked these questions and continued trying my best to tear her down as I tore myself down, the wish of being just like Mary-Kate and Ashley with their perceived closeness long forgotten.

....

I stayed this way, tearing our relationship apart piece by piece and crying myself to sleep at night after praying for a "better" body, until college. When I went away to college, I didn't see Leah every day, and the heart truly grew fonder. I started meeting women who were funny, smart, kind, and beautiful. Women who have become lifelong friends of mine, and while I didn't love myself yet, I knew I loved them. Then one day it hit me: these qualities that I loved so much in my friends had been in my sister all along, but I had been too jealous and angry to see that. I knew that to be better to Leah, I had to be better to myself. I began being honest in my therapy sessions in college, hashing out all my insecurities, and owning up to all my bullshit in regard to our relationship. In those sessions, I was vulnerable in a way that I never allowed myself to be publicly before. The counselor and I spoke of my jealousy as a fact, instead of as a dirty word I was once desperate to avoid. We were as frank with each other as I am being with you.

Jealousy makes us all vulnerable and scared. We recognize that it is often painful, unnecessary, and gets us nowhere, but we feel it anyway—and for the smallest and biggest reasons. As emotional human beings, we sometimes can't help how we feel or when we feel it. But that fear, of naming jealousy and other toxic ways we can harm the ones we love, can't be conquered until we acknowledge and face it.

....

I decided that after graduating from college in 2013, I would face the damage I had done and work to be the sister who Leah had deserved all along. When I got home, I went right to work on our relationship. I started telling her I loved her more, complimenting her fashion choices, and apologizing for all the things I had said—both to and about her—while we were growing up. We wouldn't get those years back, but our new memories were worthwhile, too. These new memories included trips to the mall, sister lunches, girls' nights, and shared secrets, but time pressed on, and so did we. In truth, we are not as close as I'd like, but my hopes do not reign supreme here. I know that Leah loves me, and I've never had to question that. The tempering of expectations is my job and mine alone. I had this grandiose dream of us being like the twins we once admired, but I broke us before we could become those twins.

I also understand that, like me, Leah is her own person with her own friends and dreams. After years spent tearing her down, I understand why we aren't suddenly as close as the twins we grew up watching. Leah has forgiven me and I have forgiven myself for the most part, but neither of us will ever be able to forget the past. In this regard, I think that what we have is what we are supposed to have. At the end of the day, I'm thankful that at least she did not decide to walk out of my life forever, even when she was well within her right to do so. I know that we will never live out my grandiose dream and that I will always be the person she loves who has hurt her. Therefore, I will take what I can get with a smile, because it could be worse. We will never have what Mary-Kate and Ashley or Tia and Tamera had, but what we do have is complicated, messy, and beautiful in its own way.

....

Leah wasn't the only person in my household growing up. I also have an older brother, Eric, who is three years older than us. We do not have a great relationship, though the reasons aren't the same as Leah's and mine. I didn't really worry too much about his "normalcy" growing up, because he was older and not a woman, so I didn't feel like there was a competition between us. I wasn't threatened by him in the same way that I felt threatened by Leah. He and I never had much in common growing up, so while I lived in our house with him, we didn't really know each other. Growing up, I made Eric a background character in my life, always there but never contributing to the development of my story in any real way. I could have made a better effort with him, but as we grew older the window for us closed as we chose different paths in life. Eric and I argue all the time, even now; our personalities just don't mesh well. To his credit, he tries to throw out olive branches more often than I do. I am kinder to others in a way that I am not with him, which is a fault I carry alone. Eric and Leah have always gotten along better, and that's perfectly fine with me, because I know that he has at least one positive relationship with one of his siblings. I say all of this because, as I mentioned earlier, I think honesty serves us best in most cases. I am no saint—just a woman trying to own her truths. My relationship with Leah matters so much to me now that trying to fix my relationship with Eric, which soured slowly over the years, feels like too much work in the midst of repairing things with my sister. In regard to the dynamic that Eric and I have, Leah is the true neutral zone. She lets me vent my frustrations about him while having the ability to explain things to me from his point of view. She's a much more levelheaded person than I am, and she forgives where I've been known to hold grudges.

I can confidently tell you that Eric and I love each other but we don't often like each other. Eric has his own demons the way humans do, and I do believe they have made our relationship, at best, tenser. This is where we are, but maybe it won't always be. He has a four-year-old daughter, Eveyah, who looks at him with stars in her eyes. My niece is one of the greatest gifts my family has been given, and when I watch her with him, I wonder what it would be like to see him that way, too. Or at best, with a clean slate. I do not have predictions for the future of our relationship, because relationships are messy and humans are messy. My mess did not start or end with him, because he is not a villain, and neither am I, because nothing is ever that cut-and-dry. I am still working out the intricacies of our relationship and the way it is both good and bad, both beautiful and ugly. There are stories I believe only he has the right to tell if and when he decides to tell them. In the meantime, I have been so focused on rewriting my relationship with Leah because there is an unspoken connection between us. We share identical DNA; she is a part of me as I am of her. I say as much knowing that it is not a real excuse for the way I have neglected and punished Eric for his past and current behavior. I do not have our relationship figured out, but I know that I am quick to anger and slow to forgive most where he is concerned.

....

As I mentioned earlier, a thing that I will always be appreciative of with regard to both Eric and Leah is that they never looked at me like I was Frankenstein's monster or a problem to be fixed, even as I looked at myself that way. I was, and I am, just Keah, their loud-laughing, nosy, music- and pop-culture-obsessed, cheesecake-loving sister. I don't have to worry about how they view me in terms of disability. I do sometimes wonder if the questions from friends and strangers alike ever embarrassed them. I am admittedly *a lot* at times, and I wonder if my having a disability ever made them uncomfortable. If I asked, they'd say no, either way, but there's comfort in knowing that there are people in the world who just don't give a damn about what others say. I never had to prove to them that I could be a good sister even with my disability. Disability shouldn't ever be something someone must negotiate or learn to accept in any relationship.

I am grateful that I never had to negotiate my disability with my family. Even when I didn't deserve her, I had Leah's approval, and even though Eric and I don't have a healthy or positive relationship, it's not because of my disability; it is because of countless other things. My disability is a one-line character in my relationship with both Eric and Leah, and that's always how it should've been, particularly with Leah. I am just sad it took me so long to realize that.

....

In 2015, I was able to interview Tia Mowry for my former employer *Cliché* magazine and tell her just how much she and her sister had meant to me and mine while we were growing up. Tia was one of the first representations in my childhood of a person and a character who loved who she was all the time. I was a shaking and crying mess when we hung up the phone. The interview felt like a career and life highlight. As an entertainment journalist, I try my best to remember that celebrities are just humans with public jobs, but I felt like I came full circle when she and I spoke. My self-love wasn't present yet, but it was bubbling beneath the surface. Just before the interview's end, I had the opportunity in a few words to thank one of the people who had positively shaped my childhood and the sister I am today. I will forever be grateful for that.

Leah and I have been through so much with each other, but before all the bad, there was so much good. Tia and Tamera were a part of the *before* and part of the innocence that came with being young and believing that the world was made of things that would bring me only joy and happiness. When I interviewed Tia, she had a cooking show and a show on Nick at Nite, and she was toying with the idea of having another kid. Now, after those shows have ended, she's thriving on her YouTube channel and has had another child. I look at the change in her life and realize that not all change is bad.

....

I am constantly changing, and so are Leah and Eric. We will not be the same people months or years from now, but growth is good and necessary. I don't know where our relationships with each other will lead when the seasons and years change, but I hope they flourish in those new places and I hope we get to grow together. At this point, the biggest moments in my life thus far have included Leah. She was there when I graduated from college, landed a literary agent, went viral, sold a book, and was asked to do TV interviews. She is one of my biggest supporters and has expressed slight frustration of her own. She told me once that she was so happy for me, genuinely, but slightly jealous of the fact that I had figured out what I loved to do and was doing it. I had never thought that I could make anyone envious, let alone the woman I spent years of my life envying, and it helped me realize that I needed to appreciate and love what I do have in my life. I am admittedly doing pretty good for a black disabled girl from a city no one has heard of.

At the risk of sounding like an inspirational quote on a greeting card, I can say that my jealousy toward my sister taught me that I was never really jealous of her, but rather of what I perceived she had that I thought I deserved. I didn't know who Leah was back then, not really. I never took the time to get to know her, because of my preconceived notions based on her appearance. I was doing to her what society had done to me, and it took my loving and accepting who I am to realize that.

In my family we believe that while friendly competition is important, it isn't necessary to tear down anyone in the process. We push each other to be better and show up to support each other at every win and loss. We are each other's biggest cheerleaders, and my siblings and family members aren't afraid to call people out when they catch them staring at me. They don't do it often, because they can gauge the situation to see if the person should be called out. (One time, Leah and I were in the mall and caught this man staring with his mouth wide open. Leah rolled her eyes before looking directly at him and said loud enough for him to hear, "Can we help you?" to which he responded with stammered words as he continued to watch me. Startled, he ran into another mall kiosk, and I felt like justice was done.) I believe that we shouldn't let anything or anyone stop us from becoming who we are, and that we should champion everyone who is in the thick of it—especially the people who have loved us unconditionally. For me, this includes the person who has been in my corner patiently waiting for me to see in myself what she has seen in me since 1991.

....

Jealousy is a funny thing. We give jealousy so much power and space in our lives. Jealousy has its own room in our homes and its favorite food in our refrigerator. I am not the person with all the answers, but I do know that I almost lost my sister to my fear, insecurity, and jealousy. I almost missed out on the beautiful woman she is becoming because I didn't think that I was beautiful. The past is such that I can't get it back, but I can be a better person for my sister and myself. I can be honest about the very real feelings I experienced in the hopes that I won't make my same mistakes once more. The best thing about our individually lived experiences is that we come out of them with an idea of how to handle them if something similar happens again. Jealousy will find me again, I'm sure of it. It will come in a different form, but my hope is that it won't last as long and that I will have a reference for how I handled it the first time.

When I first began trying to be a better twin to Leah, I was racked with guilt. Here was this person I loved whose life I believed I made a living hell. Was I responsible for every bad memory, moment, and experience in her life up until 2013? I thought so, and these thoughts led me to constantly apologize, because when I looked at Leah, all I saw was the young, sad girl I once had been. I was the antagonist in her story and I had to reckon with that, even with her reassurances that I wasn't as detrimental to her as my imagination dreamt up. We have spent a lot of time discussing my past behavior, and Leah has been patient and kind to me as I work through my guilt and I mourn the loss of years spent riddled with anger and jealousy. She stood by me as I grieved the body I'd never have and learned to embrace the body I was given instead. I didn't deserve Leah until the tail end of 2013. I didn't deserve her love, compassion, trust, or kindness, but I received it anyway. For twenty-seven years she gave me her best and deepest love, the kind of love someone can have only for her twin, and I didn't even notice. Now, though, I won't allow myself to waste any more time with guilt or jealousy. I will return that love to Leah and I will be better to her—one day at a time and one word at a time.

IS THIS THING ON?

··

I am a black disabled woman. I am not handicapable, differently abled, special needs, or any other iteration of disabled that says anything but the word *disabled*. When I say as much, I am speaking for myself and myself alone. My thoughts on the matter are not the case for every person with disabilities, because we are not monolithic. Some people like or use the terms above, but I do not. What I am about to say might make some of you uncomfortable, but discomfort is imperative here. Discomfort has made a lot of things better in the long run.

When I stopped caring about the comfort of able-bodied people with regard to the language used about my disability, I felt free for the first time in my life. You see, these other synonyms for *disability* were created because the word *disabled* often makes able-bodied people more uncomfortable than it makes those of us with disabilities. The Disability History Museum has this to say: "The present examination of disability has no need for the medical language of symptoms and diagnostic categories. Disability studies looks to different kinds of signifiers and the identification of different kinds of syndromes for its material. The elements of interest here are the linguistic conventions that structure the meanings assigned to disability and the patterns of response to disability that emanate from, or are attendant upon, those meanings." I agree that the nature of disability and the idea of diagnosis are changing and that language is vastly important to those of us who identify as people who have disabilities. *Disabled*, in the eyes of many, is a dirty word because it shines light on the differences of our world, and when we acknowledge difference, we must acknowledge privilege—and that opens a whole other can of worms.

The thing that even the most "progressive" people forget is that language is as important to the act of identification as anything else. How we live our lives, navigate the world, and communicate with each other have more to do with language than people might believe. I am not talking about the spoken word, because there are millions of people in our world who do not speak aloud but who use nonverbal language to communicate, whether that's American or British Sign Language or nonverbal cues and so forth. But *communication* is the one thing we all use. Language will forever be a way that one human can relate to another, because even if we cannot speak the same language, the desire and need to communicate with people and find other humans who share our interests is an almost universal one.

When I was growing up, *disability* wasn't a part of my lexicon, because I did not want it to be part of me at all. If I talked about it, that made it real, and I wanted desperately for my disability to be some cruel joke God was playing until I learned a lesson and he took it away—like in the movies. If you've ever seen the movie *Penelope* with Christina Ricci—in which Penelope is cursed with the nose of a pig through no fault of her own and has to live with it—you'll understand what I mean. Penelope breaks the curse by the end of the movie, but I knew I'd never have such luck. So, apart from the time when I was eight and begged my mom to ride horses and she graciously researched a facility for disabled kids, I stayed as far away from anything disability-related as I could. I recoiled at the mere mention of it because I was petrified at being thought of as *other*. I tried my best to play it cool in public spaces, but the fact that disability made me different consumed my every waking thought. That's the funny thing about hating something you can't change: you can aim for aloofness, but that lends itself to obsession and frustration that people absolutely pick up on.

I was uncomfortable with my existence. Everything from my physical appearance to the sound of my voice made me feel uneasy, as if someone were going to verbally attack me at any moment and whatever that person said about me would hold merit. I was afraid of finding new things to hate about myself by way of someone else's words. I liken this to that same discomfort that some white people feel at the mention of white privilege and the confrontation of the truth behind it. No one likes it when a truth they know in the deepest parts of themselves is pointed out by someone else. It makes us vulnerable, and vulnerability is scary because it isn't as controllable as we'd like it to be.

We all have had those moments when our best friends or loved ones tell us something we need to hear even when we don't want to hear it. It is easy to remember how we block out their advice and words only to return later and begrudgingly admit that they were right. The discomfort of sitting in the truth and trying to decide whether or not to accept it is the same type of discomfort with which I spent most of my life. My uncomfortable truth was that I had a physical disability that people could see or judge; they could take one look at me and decide whether I was good enough to be in their lives, clubs, or friend groups. There were years when I put my happiness in the hands of strangers and acquaintances by giving them the power to decide whether I was having a bad day via a simple laugh or a point my way. (A good day was when I knew they were staring and laughing but I was too winded from walking to concentrate on that.) When you relinquish power the way that I did, you forget what it feels like to hold it in your hands—or that you had any to call your own in the first place. Power is tricky to navigate; to understand it, you have to lay the groundwork for what makes you powerful in the first place.

I have a visible disability, though I have a few invisible disabilities and illnesses, too—chronic migraines, seasonal depression, and anxiety. But for now, we'll focus on the one you can see. I have cerebral palsy, and it's fine, most days. Sometimes I want to scream and cry when my knee locks up or my hip and leg start hurting out of the blue. I get angry when I struggle to do what could be seen as an easy thing, like opening a bag of chips, zipping a zipper, or picking up something with both hands. I tire after walking long distances because I subconsciously hold my breath while walking, and sometimes this makes me want to disappear. I, too, feed into the idealization of youth and the ability to do things "young people should be able to do" despite the fact that I know that's ableist bullshit. As I said, there's a lot left for me to learn and unlearn.

Ableism is defined as discrimination and social prejudice against people with disabilities. What I spent most of my life with is internalized ableism. I fed into those prejudices and believed them to be true. Now I want to shout that I am disabled from the rooftops. There is a point to prove to people who don't think that we should care so much about identity. These days, there is all this rhetoric about how identity politics is ruining things but not enough about how satisfying and how affirming identity and identifiers (a way to name the identities one person associates with) make communities of people who would be considered invisible otherwise. After years spent trying to avoid any conversation surrounding my disability, I want the world to know that I am disabled and proud. There is power in this identity—power and relief. The relief of worrying less about the opinions that strangers have of my body? Of being free to identify how I want and live how I please? It feels like a dream that I do not want to wake up from.

No one wants to feel like an animal at the zoo on display without choice, not even those animals at the zoo. I find that the worst parts of CP, aside from the aches and pains, are the stares from adults, as if they've never seen someone limp before and were not taught any sense of respect or decorum. I am obviously much kinder with children and tell them stories that make them smile, because they are adorable. My issue lies with adults who stare with their mouths open and have the nerve to be upset when they catch me on the right day and I say something. Before I accepted my CP, I would cower in shame at their staring and apologize with my eyes for existing. Although the shame is gone now, the frustration and agitation will likely be alive and well in me for as long as I live or for as long as people keep staring. My frustration and agitation in these moments are emotions I will not apologize for. I have been actively trying to be a nicer, more considerate person in recent years because I spent too long being unhappy and angry, but I feel strongly that there is no reason to apologize for my irritation toward the zoo-like treatment I often receive when I am just trying to live my life. Regardless, I will never allow that irritation to make me turn inward and blame or hate myself again.

What I didn't know earlier, but am grateful that I know now, is that my cerebral palsy is an integral part of who I am and how I navigate the world. In my refusal to acknowledge this, I was denying the world and myself a glimpse of who I really am. All that time wasted hiding away, when I could've embraced my girl CP and the word *disabled* and found unapologetic happiness sooner. I was embarrassed of disability, of being disabled, and of other disabled people. My thought processes were that if able-bodied people discussed my disability, then they would see me as inferior—and I already saw myself as inferior. I didn't want them to as well. I would rather have been ignored than pitied, but I was never ignored, not then or now. The only thing that has changed is the way I feel about myself. Pity was my greatest fear and my biggest foe, but now I can confidently say that I do not care about it, because I know how I feel about myself.

....

Pity as a practice is an interesting thing. It finds its way into a lot of conversations about disability. Society often prides itself on its ability to pity disabled bodies and uses them as a warning of how bad life can be. In such instances, we cease being people at all in favor of being tools and reasons to appreciate the hardships in others' lives. I hated being pitied by friends of my family or by teachers who would talk to me slowly and condescendingly, as if I weren't able to understand them otherwise. They were always puzzled when I would respond without issue, leaving the onus on me to awkwardly laugh it off. I hated being pitied, but I also felt sorry for myself more often than not. I internalized every slow speaker, every dismissal of my autonomy by people who refused to really listen when I spoke to them. They became a sign that this was what my life would be forever: pity and infantilization. That is no longer my life, and that is what I am most grateful for. Still, I wish I could have found a polite way of bringing it up back then, of showing these people how harmful even the best of their intentions could be.

Pity is not a thing I need even now. I gave pity so much power to control my daily life. The lesson that took me the longest to learn is that as a disabled person, what I need in place of pity, which does absolutely nothing to advance the community, are my rights, respect, and opportunity.

Opportunity is another imperative part of the conversation about identifiers, because I have received many opportunities that other people with disabilities have not. There is privilege in opportunity. Privilege influences opportunity and vice versa. Yes, privilege, that pesky little word from earlier, is necessary to confront in order for true equality across community, class, race, and ability to be possible. The recognition of privileges and the power structure behind them is one that many have tried to make sense of but have failed, because it is a complicated subject; as a nonexpert, I can tell you only what I know and leave the rest up to you. Privilege is the advantage or immunity given to a special group of people or a person. Being that we live in an able-bodied-centric and white-leaning society, white able-bodied people have privileges that I do not. Privileges like being able to walk around stores without being followed or having people assume that you have stolen something, as happened to me my freshman year of college when I was leaving a Walmart with three white friends. Privileges like your heart not racing the moment you see a police officer, not because you did anything wrong but because society has taught you that your skin color makes you a target. Privileges like walking into a building with broken handrails and no short-term seating for when your body needs to rest and being fine. There are also the global privileges of whiteness in the workforce, in housing markets, in government positions, and more. But I digress.

But this is not an essay being written from a high horse (though I do love horses). I have privileges, too, just not as many as a white, straight, able-bodied male—as evidenced by the fact that we live in a patriarchy filled with mediocre white men who do nothing but fail up. Nevertheless, I have a mother, a sister, a cousin, and an aunt who take me to doctor's appointments and drop me off at airports when I need to travel. They shuffle me to stores when I need things, and my mother fought for me when I was too young to fight for myself in our educational system. This is a privilege I acknowledge because I know many disabled and able-bodied people don't have the support system I do, and my support system allowed me to get where I am today. What I try my best to do is remember that the opportunities I have had are not only because of hard work (though I have worked my ass off), but also because I was able to say yes, knowing that I could look to my family and friends for both emotional and financial support if need be. When we acknowledge our privilege, we can work together to dismantle a system in which privilege doesn't shut out the under-represented but rather casts a hand down to pull someone else up.

I have been given the opportunity to tell my stories and the stories of people like me. I do not take this opportunity for granted, because I know that it may all fade away or may mean that I am the first disabled black woman whose work people may read. That's why honesty is so important to me. There is a responsibility in being the first, and I try not to think of it until after the work is finished, but it creeps up on me from time to time. I want to do justice to my sisters-in-arms and our stories. I feel that it is my duty to introduce my stories to willing listeners and also make it clear that I am not the only voice or the final decision maker. What is written here is simply the opinion and experiences of one person, not law. I am just a black disabled woman from a small town no one knows the name of who started being honest with herself so that she could be honest with the world. What I want to make sure I tell you, and what I will continue to tell people across publications, podcasts, and TV interviews, is that *disabled* is not a dirty word. Say it with me, please. Disabled *is not a dirty word*. Feels good, right? Saying the words is so important to the process of shifting preconceived notions. Trust me, I said this exact thing every day until I truly believed it. Then I started working inward to adjust what I had once believed about disability.

Whether it is visible or invisible, disability is nothing to pity. That is what I hope you take from my work. The physical disability is neither as bad nor as beneficial as it is made out to be by people who swear that those of us with cerebral palsy are all gaming the system. My cerebral palsy is a firecracker. She demands a lot of me and my body, and she slows me down, but she is also part of me, so when she inflicts pain on me, she is inflicting the same pain on herself. My wins are hers as well. It is a strange thing to think about having never lived in a body without her; I know that not everyone has a part of their body actively working for and against her at the same time. After reading *Freshwater* by Akwaeke Emezi I think I understand us both better, and now I want the world to understand us better, too. When you turn to your friends or loved ones, or when you see a character on TV with a disability, I hope you remember these words. Together we can change the attitudes about and surrounding disability, as long as we remember that pity helps no one—while empathy, love, and a willingness to fight help everyone.

....

What I have noticed in my years on earth is that disability is often defined or regarded as if something were wrong with the disabled person inherently. However, such a viewpoint is a product of perspective. The only thing wrong with disability is that we live in a world that's inaccessible to anyone who does not have a thin frame or the full use of their body without chronic illness. If we are made to go through the world every day knowing that it was not designed with our bodies in mind or with our human rights at the ready, we deserve the chance and the space to identify how we wish and to be proud of our identifiers, to embrace the communities that welcomed us when society essentially turned us away. I love my identifiers for this reason: because they are mine in every way, even when they mean that I am distancing myself from what is perceived to be normal. "Normal" is a harmful idea that sustains itself by dictating rules of what should and should not be. In many circles, my mild disability grants me access to opportunities that people with more severe disabilities do not have access to.

Opportunity lends itself to the practice of reclamation. Many people within the disability community, excluding myself, have decided to reclaim the word *cripple*. I have decided not to do so, because it is one of those words I will personally never feel comfortable using or having used in any way toward me. I remember hearing it as a child on TV, when it was used as a taunt from one child to another. I didn't know what it meant, exactly, but I had the intuitiveness to guess that it was not a compliment. It popped up again in my early high school years when anonymous question sites like Formspring were popular and I received a handful of questions calling me a cripple or asking why I was one. This furthered a negative view of myself at a formative age and time in my life. However, I recognize and cheer on those wishing to reclaim the word, because it is their right to do what they wish with the words that have had an impact on them. There is power and excitement in reclaiming things that were once used to hurt or demean you.

In fact, after #DisabledAndCute received some backlash because of the community's history with the word *cute* implying infantilization, I explained to naysayers how I was reclaiming *cute* in the way that others had reclaimed *cripple* before me. I reminded them that, at the end of the day, the hashtag was created using the words that made me feel comfortable, and that if it bothered them too much, they could decide not to participate. I feel the same way about the word *disabled* and its usage by those of us who choose to use it. Our choice is just that—ours—and it is only fair that we get a say in how we identify ourselves and each other, and how we are identified by society.

Despite the fact that I feel this way, I in no way think I am speaking for anyone but myself and the community members to whom I have spoken and who feel the same way as I do. There has been a push by some members within the disability community in recent years to move away from the word *disabled* to a more palatable word. What I have noticed is that these requests often come from parents of people with disabilities. They assume what makes them uncomfortable in terms of vernacular makes their children uncomfortable, too, but the only way to know for sure is for them to ask, and that doesn't happen as often as it should. That is an example of infantilization in and of itself.

The moral of the story is this: disabled people deserve the chance to choose how we identify, because with identity comes power—more accurately, the ability to take our power back from the people who took it away in the first place, those who made us believe that they knew what was best for us more than we could or did. Identity and identifiers mean freedom. We are free from the expectations of others when we choose to be fully who we are and choose how to label ourselves. The freedom in choice can shift the conversation and make the world a place where all people can choose how they are seen.

Part of identity for me has always included accessibility and the necessity of it. We don't talk enough about comfort and accessibility. The conversation hasn't fully hit mainstream spaces, because they operate under the assumption that it is never an issue for anyone occupying space in the rooms where conversations about inclusion and representation happen. Comfort and accessibility deserve to go hand in hand, but often accessibility feels like folklore, a fable told many years ago that loses its magic when you learn that it should be real and isn't a fable at all, just something a group of people deserve but do not have in the way they should. Accessibility isn't necessary just for people with permanent disabilities; it's also necessary for people with temporary disabilities like broken legs and arms who have not had years to adapt to a world that thinks so little about people whose bodies are not fully functioning constantly. Accessibility can be for fat bodies, for both able-bodied and disabled bodies with regard to chairs that are designed with thin or thinner bodies in mind. At some point, in all our lives, whether able-bodied or disabled, accessibility is or will be important. If it is hard to think of others, think of yourself, but understand that something has to change. So, in making accessibility a core aspect of my identifiers, I hope to shine light on its necessity.

The importance of identifiers is not just for my disabled identity. I identified myself as a black woman during my childhood. I was always proud of my black skin and the history behind blackness. I knew from an early age that my black was beautiful and I never questioned it. The people in my family and the people in my life were black, beautiful, intelligent, and cool, the kind of natural cool that isn't taught or learned but understood. I had pride in them long before I had it in myself, so I never questioned the outward common trait we shared. However, I understood that my blackness was considered a strike against me in society—in fact, in every system that society influences. This has always been the case, but especially now, when we watch the killings of black men and women by the police on the nightly news and know that justice will not be served. I know all the more that my blackness is a strike against me when I see that the murders of black trans women and black lesbians receive little to no fanfare, no news coverage, and no justice.

I am a disabled black woman but I am also a feminist—a proud one. I am a sister, a daughter, an aunt, a niece, a friend, and a cousin, and I am a human being. These identifiers matter to me as much as they would to anyone who identifies in the same way, because we are often asked to reckon with our humanity. A way to do so is to accept who and what we are with the hope that we will live our truths happily and without worry. At least, that is my hope. As much as identifiers are a way to freedom and power, they are also important because they are places to belong. Even with the support system I have, it is nice to know people who understand my specific experiences not just because they love and care for me, but because they have lived the same experiences, too. I love my family and friends, but there are things they don't understand about physical disability because they do not have one. There are things that the disability community at large does not understand about those of us who have a lot of able-bodied people in our lives by choice. That is why I sometimes compartmentalize the groups of people that I love when I deem it necessary and helpful for everyone involved. I can come to my people for different things based on what I know they have experienced, and it feels like we are a well-oiled, loving machine that way. I have learned first from the lessons of others. I think we all do.

Before we begin a formal education, we learn the world and our places within it from our parents, guardians, friends, or loved ones. We are not born knowing the ways of the world. We are taught specific things based on community by family and friends. In black communities we are taught to always keep our hands where they can be seen if and when we are pulled over by cops. We are taught to respond to their questions with "Yes, sir" and "No, sir" and "Yes, ma'am" and "No, ma'am" and pray that we make it home safely. We know that it is necessary to code-switch, which means changing the way we speak in casual or business settings. We are also taught by history, first in the classrooms and again outside them. (In the classroom, I learned that Christopher Columbus discovered America. On TV, I learned that Christopher Columbus was a mass murderer and a liar.) We learn history, in many ways, because we cannot go forward until we acknowledge where we have been. Even with the knowledge of where we have been, we sometimes find history repeating itself, because despite what we know, power is in the hands of those wishing to keep racism and hatred alive, hoping to repeat the worst acts of this nation's past.

....

Under the current US administration, we are seeing pride in white nationalism and racism pushed to the forefront and championed with vigor. In the spirit of honesty, I can say that I am worried I will not see the same for people like me in my lifetime. We are not allowed that same pride; we will never have that same sense of security. Especially when we have the cops called on us for selling water, barbecuing, going to the pool, and using coupons at the store, among other seemingly inconsequential things. Those acts are the identifiers the racists who call the cops take pride in, the ones that make them feel heard and seen after years spent having to tuck away their hatred in mixed company. I think they prove that there shouldn't

be pride in the identities that work to demean and harm other people, especially by people who embody some perceived difference to
mean they are better than someone else because of it. There was an
instance in which racist white people stuck their black roommate's
toothbrushes up their anuses and smeared blood on her items to
make her sick, and then they ended up not being charged with a hate
crime. In fact, the defendants' lawyers explained away the episode as
a misguided decision. There have been nooses stuck on trees where
black students gather at universities, as well as an instance in which
a young black man was found rolled up in a gymnasium mat, and we
were expected to believe that he was the cause of his own death. It is
clear that there is still so much work left to do while showcasing the
privileges of whiteness and the unjust systems under which black,
brown, disabled, and LGBTQ+ people are forced to live—especially
for those of us at multiple intersections of identity. The work of identity and reclamation, and the work and fight toward true freedom,
can feel never-ending at times—but it is always necessary.

A lot of people with disabilities have muddied histories with
nondisabled people. We weren't granted any real rights or protections until a year before I was born, in 1990, and after the passing
of bills that infringed on those rights by able-bodied people. I think
it is easy and fair to be distrustful of the people looking to strip you
of your livelihood. The ADA Education and Reform Act—which
passed in the US House of Representatives as HR620 in 2018 and is
designed to roll back the rights of disabled people—would require
that people with disabilities who wish to report access barriers in
buildings and public spaces become essentially code experts, give
notice to the appropriate owners, and then wait six months or longer
for the business or government agency to make "substantial progress." And that doesn't even guarantee that the issues in question will

be fixed! The power is often never in our hands; we often have to fight for what should already be our rights as citizens, and when we protest proposed harmful changes to things like Medicaid, we seldom receive any support or genuine media attention, while risking our lives in the fight to stay alive. The disability community and the black community have that fight in common.

There will be more work to do and more to say than just loudly proclaiming who we are and where we belong, but the proclamation is important now in our current cultural landscape. To proclaim that I am and you are a specific person with specific experiences in the world is to simply say that you, in all that you are, love yourself despite living in a world that wishes you feel otherwise. There is reason to celebrate even on the days when it may feel impossible to. Often the work involves simply trying and failing and knowing that when you fail you will wait a beat and try again. In many ways, the try-and-fail method follows the identifiers' process. We can try out identities and find communities to call our own. Some last forever and some don't, but we never stop learning about ourselves along the way.

This is not easy work, because identity is a nuanced thing that can change or shift whenever we see fit, and that's why it is important in the first place: because it deserves to be respected as a thing that is ours alone but that we choose to share with the world. The same can be said for self-love. I think figuring out what you love about yourself is a big part of identity and the deciding factor in what you choose to identify as. Loving yourself is an everyday task, and some days you will not. Weeks will come and go and you will feel like you were hit by a truck, because the world can be an exhausting one. But at the risk of sounding cheesy, I can tell you that what's important is to keep going and to hold on to who you are when the world is trying to tear you down just for being you.

After you do the work of self-identification, of living your life as the person you want to be, the work of fighting for the communities and people you claim starts. In the era of resistance, we organize a lot of marches and protests, and they are necessary but often inaccessible. I hope that we can also move into financial support of smaller organizations fighting the good fight for policy and structural changes needed to help protect the rights and livelihoods of the marginalized. If the money isn't there, that's understandable. I don't often have extra money to give to organizations, so instead I pass the mic and share on my platforms the voices of those who need to get a message out.

The resistance can't be solely about pussy hats (which are exclusionary of women who do not have vaginas) and photo ops at marches and protests with clever signs. As a black woman, I understand that my ancestors had to fight not only to survive under the shackles of slavery but also to keep the cultures and traditions of blackness alive. Black people worked so hard for us to have equality that the civil rights movement was born. There are people who died for my well-being whose names I will never know, and the sadness in that fact is soothed only by the fact that I can wear our mutual identity with pride. I understand that the disabled women and men before me also fought to give me the rights I have today with the Americans with Disabilities Act of 1990. This is a fact that keeps me fighting every single day. The civil rights movement was still active when my mother was born in 1965, and my rights as a disabled person were granted only a year before I was born. These injustices were not in some faraway past but in our recent pasts, our lifetimes, the lifetimes of our parents and grandparents. Sure, we've come a long way. I can eat at the same table as my best friends. We can attend concerts of our favorite bands and exist in the same room and under the same perceived rules. I can sit anywhere I want on public transportation; I can access flights for the ability to travel for work or leisure; I had access to a college education and completed college to earn a degree; and I had the tools and support necessary to write this book. Still, we have such a long way to go for true equality for everyone. I often feel that the least I can do to thank the people whom I will never know, and those I do, is to feel pride and proclaim my identities so that their deaths and struggles will not have been in vain.

There is an old saying that goes, "When I eat, we all eat." Or just "We all eat." This is about what I said earlier about reaching down and pulling someone up. I am always going to pay it forward and send opportunities to people when I can't fulfill them or when I am just not the right person to try. I know who "we" are because I know who I am, and I learned who I was through the communities I identify with and language I have chosen to use.

In the act of choosing how we identify by choosing words both old and new, we are also choosing whom we will fight for and fight with. I am a black disabled woman. *Disabled* is the word with which I have chosen to walk through my life thus far. Maybe one day that will change or maybe it won't, but the word will always be important in my fight for my communities—all of them. The feminist, black, female, and disabled communities still have so much work to do when it comes to recognizing and respecting each other, but as that work is taking place, I will continue to name and claim them because they keep me when I have trouble keeping myself. The great thing about belonging to various communities is that by doing so we actively choose each other as we choose ourselves and the people we are and who we hope to be. What we know about language is that it can be considered a first step to adjusting preconceived notions and identifiers, the stones to show language the way. Who do you get to be while you live in the world? Are you a woman? A man? A gender-nonconforming person? Whoever you are, are you happy with who you get to be? I ask because at the end of the day it is what we all deserve. Self-identification will not save the world, but we deserve to find out how change will make the world a better place. After all, we live in a world that could use a bit of change.

POP CULTURE & ME:
A (SOMETIMES) UNREQUITED LOVE STORY

I grew up hating mirrors. I made them my enemy. When I used them in the mornings, I would rush, looking up only long enough to make sure nothing was on my face. I began turning away while brushing my teeth, closing my eyes while my mother did my hair, and washing my face with my eyes trained on the sink. In stores, I perfected the passing glance, though those always came with a sly internal mocking of whatever I saw. I dreaded having to see myself in all my imperfections, so I changed my personality to fit whomever I was with and prayed to wake up in a new body every night. I toyed with my first thoughts of suicidal ideation, deciding that living wasn't living at all if I had to do so in a disabled body. I taught myself to hate me better than anyone else ever could.

Growing up, I had much healthier representations on TV and in film than in my own mirror. I saw a plethora of black faces in these mediums. There was my favorite, *Cinderella*, with Brandy and the late Whitney Houston. I watched in awe as Brandy arrived at the ball in the blue gown I had previously seen in pictures on only a white animated woman. In this made-for-TV movie, Brandy in her braids and glowing black skin is the center of attention, the love interest.

Whitney Houston is her fairy godmother, and they sing together beautifully about how "impossible things are happening every day." I remember it being the first time I believed in the magic of dreaming, though I wouldn't realize the full impact of this movie on my sense of self until years later. As I watched, I felt like I could be a love interest, too, that I was as beautiful as Cinderella—or rather, that I would be someday. Since I saw this version before I ever saw the animated original, I am a little biased, but I believe it is the best *Cinderella*.

After that, there was the nineties remake of *Annie*, which I unapologetically love to this day. In this remake, Audra McDonald plays Grace Farrell, the assistant to and eventual love interest of Oliver Warbucks, played by Victor Garber. My love of Grace hinged on her beautiful voice and that same glow I had seen in Brandy. Grace was a love interest, too, but more than that, she was someone the main character loved without pause, not because he had to but because he chose to. I was desperate for a love like that even when I was young, desperate to be sure I was loved outside familial obligation. I think that it is a hard desire to explain when you live with multiple representations of yourself, but I can tell you that when you have none, you get lonely, and the first thing you begin to question is your worth.

After those representations, there was Whoopi Goldberg as "Mother Gooseberg" in the TV movie *Mother Goose: A Rappin' and Rhymin' Special*. In the animated film, black and brown faces were everywhere, black and brown boys and girls who didn't question their looks, who weren't forced to address their ethnicities as if they needed to be explained. They were young children with dreams, in classic children's stories reimagined and reinvigorated. I felt spoiled by all that I had for representation as a child, and I think it is why I am able to long for even more improved versions today.

My childhood was filled with joy and wonder because of my

ability to see and know stories like these. I felt seen and heard without really knowing what impact these depictions would have on me until I was much older. These stories and these people were my introduction to popular culture, and what a beautiful and exciting introduction it was. As a child I marveled at the black people in their bodies on my TV and VHS tapes. Bodies that were nothing like mine in the way that they could and would pick up things with their hands without pause, run and walk long distances, but still, we shared the same skin, and so I loved them a little more for it, cheered a little harder when they reached their happily-ever-after endings. These movies allowed me to love my black skin long before the world would try to convince me not to. I know that we all have a tendency to romanticize the past, and maybe I am doing so, but I think of that time of movies and television as the years that allowed me to be unapologetically black. I saw that same energy reflected back to me so often that I never had to question it, and I didn't even think about it as a thing I could lose.

As the landscape of television and popular culture changed, so did I. At the close of the nineties we saw fewer black people on our TV screens, and as a result I was left to find ways to connect to white and nonblack characters like Rory Gilmore and Lane Kim on *Gilmore Girls*, the characters in *Dawson's Creek*, *Everwood*, *The OC*, and *Gossip Girl*. There were also kids' shows like *Zoey 101*, *Lizzie McGuire*, *Even Stevens*, and the like. I did not take the time to examine what impact watching shows with majority-white characters would have on me as I was watching them. Aside from *That's So Raven* and *Sister, Sister*, what I consumed during the nineties and early aughts was white-centered media. I watched white teenagers misbehave, fall in and out of love, and deal with drugs and guns on *The OC*, *The Hills*, *Laguna Beach*, and *The City*. In all fairness, I was young and

I just gravitated toward what was popular, which happened to be majority-white TV and film. It wasn't that I sought out whiteness but that whiteness was usually the only option for me to enjoy. But as we often do when we are older and hopefully wiser, I now wonder why I felt such a pull toward these shows when they were among others on a list too long to mention. The only answer I can come up with is that I loved them because they reflected back to me an unwavering longing for more. The longing I felt when watching them was a longing only for their characters' ability to travel, their closets of clothes, their love lives, and their financial stability. Of course, I am going to be honest and tell you that I still want these things, but I think that a part of me bought into the idea that in order to have it all, I would have to be as close to whiteness as possible. The idea was flawed for a variety of reasons, but mostly because I would absolutely have lost myself in the process.

Don't get me wrong, I loved seeing myself in these characters and I loved these shows, but after high school, I became more aware of what I was not seeing. This is not to say that I didn't watch majority-white shows anymore. In fact, there were some MTV shows, *Glee*, *Pretty Little Liars*, and a few more with some people of color sprinkled in. What changed after high school was the realization that if I, like many other black people, was able to see myself in white characters, why weren't white execs and showrunners able to see themselves in people who looked like me in order to give us the attention and agency these white and nonblack characters had? And it wasn't as though nonblack characters had the best story lines anyway. That's the thing about fighting for scraps: you don't even realize that the scraps are useless until you're close enough to see the imperfections. I saw some nonblack people of color on some of my favorite white-led shows, but I wouldn't say that Lane had what she deserved in the later seasons of *Gilmore Girls*. The writing of her and her resulting life was disappointing back then. Regardless, despite the positive changes toward inclusion being made now, I still find myself asking this very question when it comes to my being disabled: When will all of me be good enough to be seen by lovers of entertainment and popular culture like myself? When can I expect someone like me to be messy and imperfect and loved still, to be rooted for and championed through mistakes, only to captivate the audience regardless?

My love for television only intensified as I grew into a woman who has enough shows each night of the week to fall in love with. Shows that now give me what the others I loved in the past did, but also with the inclusion that they were missing. I love that our entertainment has changed with the times as we learn and grow as a society. That is the magic of entertainment. I refuse to be one of those writers who scoff at the idea of watching TV or doing anything besides reading historical books or what have you. I am a black woman who loves watching *The Fosters* (before and after it ended) and NBC's *Good Girls* on Monday. Tuesdays are for *The Flash* and *iZombie* on the CW and *Younger* on TV Land, because who doesn't love forty-year-olds pretending to be twenty-five and superheroes and zombie consultants/medical examiners? There was also *Shadowhunters* and *Kevin (Probably) Saves the World* (before they were unjustly canceled). Some of these shows conflict with each other, so DVR is my best friend. On Wednesdays, I rest, but Thursday is for the Shondaland empire, *The Good Place*, *Superstore*, and *Will and Grace*. Fridays are for *Bring It!* on Lifetime and *Jane the Virgin*. I have a real soft spot for *Jane the Virgin* because I love Gina Rodriguez (and because I once got to interview Justin Baldoni, who plays Rafael—*swoon*). Since *Orphan Black* had its series finale, my weekends are clear, apart from *Killing Eve* on BBC America, which stars Sandra Oh. *Killing Eve* is one of the best shows on television right now. The kinds of shows I love are the ones that just keep being able to reinvent themselves. Netflix is another thing entirely. I watch *Stranger Things, Grace and Frankie, One Day at a Time, Dear White People, Alexa & Katie, Bojack Horseman,* and more. If I am not binge-watching those shows when they are live on the streaming site, I aim to read and write on the weekends—but TV still manages to reign supreme.

....

To understand where I want us to go, I should take you back to a time before, when I didn't know what I wanted and when I didn't like who I was. When I didn't long to see myself even in TV shows, because I used TV to pretend I didn't exist—that, instead, I was in my body just until another one came along and I could transform into a person worthy of the lives of the characters I loved. As a child, I didn't know many disabled people or children, and the truth is, I didn't want to. I feared what knowing other people like me would mean. I spent most of my adolescence trying to steer clear of other disabled people and trying desperately to convince able-bodied people that I wasn't like them, "them" being other disabled people. I felt the need to prove my worthiness, to prove that I deserved to live among able-bodied people, as if I were a member of an alien species they would soon fear if they didn't accept me. Once I reached my middle school years and realized what a disability was and that I had one, I panicked. The only other disabled people I saw were kids with mental disabilities who needed a special education. As bad as it sounds, I still felt like an alien, so when my friends made offhand comments, I let them, so that they didn't think I was one of those disabled people. I know better now, but I did not then. I did not care about feminism or intersectionality, about being a human with enough decency to know that my shame made me no better. I did not know that I was only harming myself under the guise of self-preservation.

Today, disability pride is at the center of my nonfiction and fiction works. I feel an urgency to be seen and to give people like me someone to see, someone to love and look to the way I did the characters of Brandy, Audra, and Whoopi years before. For me, pop culture has always been about the people we see and the stories we tell even outside visual mediums. Still, as I got older, I realized that seeing my black skin on-screen was no longer enough to make me proud of who I was, because I realized what I wasn't seeing: disabled bodies. Like it or not, popular culture shapes the way we see the world, each other, and ourselves. Popular culture shifts and shapes the conversations around disability, and for so long, disability has been associated with shame and anger, shock and horror. There are films like *Me Before You* and *Million Dollar Baby* that insist we would rather die than live; there are movies like *Everything, Everything* with magic cures or "Surprise! I was never sick" endings. There are TV shows in which physically disabled characters' biggest dreams are for them to walk again, as in the hit TV shows *Star* and *Glee*. In the latter, Artie, played by Kevin McHale (an able-bodied man), wishes to walk again, and he does so, dancing excitedly, only to wake up and realize it was a dream. At some point in the series, there is even talk of a device that will allow him to walk again, until the device breaks and jokes follow shortly thereafter. On *Glee* and other TV shows, disability is both a joke and a horror, and that isn't the kind of representation we deserve. When I began researching the number of disabled writers in writers' rooms, I could not find a reputable number (aside from a few occasional consultants who had been hired). This reality saddens me, and I hope I am not alone in this. An entire community is left out of film and TV mediums created to showcase the world, to tell stories that are supposed to make people feel something: happiness, sadness, relief, understood, or a mixture of all four. What are disabled people supposed to feel when we continue not to see ourselves in these stories? When we don't see our stories in the way we deserve, because we are not in the writers' room, our absence ensuring that our stories are not even a thought?

Here's the thing: I can promise you that there are disabled people in writers' rooms, but they do not disclose this fact, because of the stigma attached to disability by the very shows and networks for which they write. The act of disclosure may also threaten their job security under the false assumption that employing disabled people who need and deserve accommodations is too costly or too much hassle. Imagine thinking that the inclusion of an entire subset and community of people to better reflect a real or imagined world is too much? The willingness to ignore the liveliness and the potential of telling stories about people with disabilities astounds me.

One of my dreams is to find myself employed in a writers' room of a show that I love with the ability to create a nuanced disabled woman who experiences the full spectrum of emotion but ultimately loves herself and doesn't make disability her every waking thought. One of my dreams is that the stigma of disability will be a thing of the past one day, a place to remember that is so far from where we are but nevertheless lives as a reminder so that we never go back. The idea that disability is punishment is reflected back to us in TV and movies, thus influencing policy and law. The fear of expressing a part of who you are for fear of backlash is a familiar concept to most marginalized people, but the cycle can be broken once we take the step of ending the stigma so that people feel comfortable disclosing and telling worthwhile stories about disability, which can then change cultural ideas and policies that negatively affect the disability community.

I am working to tell these very stories for myself first, because hopefully when these stories come to fruition, people like me won't have to grow up questioning their worth, their beauty, and their importance. There is a necessity in critiquing the things we love, because critique can help foster necessary change. Pop culture—film, television, music, art—is an everlasting love of mine, and I want it to be the best it can be. The change needs to happen in writers' rooms, but it also needs to happen in crews on the sets of TV shows and movies, in studios where music is made and in galleries where art is curated, and on magazines' editorial boards (and in their other departments, too). The necessity is not just about disabled people being in front of the camera but behind it, too, working in all aspects of entertainment, so that our stories can be told to the world across media.

....

Representation is so important because it shapes the way we see ourselves and how we are seen. In every identity, there are negative stereotypes, but for black people specifically, these stereotypes have long since infiltrated popular culture and shaped the way that we are seen in the mainstream. Until recently, we were seen only as the help, criminals, sassy best friends, and one-dimensional people. We were and sometimes still are relegated to nonspeaking dramatic roles, the few lines of encouragement to the white lead that he needs before he takes the big leap and reemerges fully formed as the hero of the story. Most black people understand that our history as a people is rich and full of leading-role stories. Blackness and black people are not monolithic.

If we look at the success of the films *Black Panther*, *Moonlight*, and *A Wrinkle in Time*, we can see that there is monetary worth in stories that aren't about slavery or black people being the embodiment of the "magical negro" trope, and that there is worth in these stories in terms of positive representation and the importance of feeling seen and heard while understanding the other contributions we have made to society. These stories are proof that whether we are unsung heroes putting men into space or kings of a hidden country whose young people are trying to figure out sexuality and the minutiae of everyday life, our stories matter. I resent the idea that we must provide this proof in the first place, when mediocre movies about middle-aged white men trying to cling to their youth are green-lit all of the time. Yet and still, we are made to do ten times more for half as much, only to get snubbed when it counts—like *Girls Trip* did when awards season rolled around. Why is our joy not enough? Why is our laughter as light through the darkest moments not proof enough of our being multifaceted entities?

This question—to which we all can guess the answer—is why I find myself concerned with the profitability of trauma and the way in which the stories of black and brown people are relegated to struggle alone. *Girls Trip* was the opposite of this idea: a story of college friends reuniting to attend the Essence Festival together, getting into trouble, having fun, and acting a little raunchy along the way. Without trauma as its thread to move the story along, I can't help but think that was why it was given the cold shoulder during awards season—and before anyone says that comedy in general is a hard sell to the Academy, *Bridesmaids* had nominations for two categories: Best Original Screenplay and Best Supporting Actress. Why should the stories of our pain and hardship be the only ones rewarded? Our joy is beautiful, too, and just as important. It should not be that we must always cry and die, reliving the trauma of physical and emotional abuse for our stories to be deemed award worthy. I know that awards are not everything, but the recognition matters when filmmakers are looking to green-light other projects and finance their next stories in order to bring new lives to the screen. Progress is remembering that breaks from pain are not only recommended but necessary, that finding the joys in life despite systemic oppression can save lives. Why don't black and brown people have the luxury of those breaks more often when we visit cinemas or relax on our couches? We say the opposite when we tell black and brown filmmakers and audiences that critical success and career stability result from telling stories of trauma alone. This indicates that only our pain is acceptable to a wide-ranging audience.

Film isn't the only perpetrator of this idea. TV in more recent years has seen a resurgence of black and brown faces in multifaceted roles that sometimes lean on trauma in order to reach a wider audience. To do this, such shows force their characters to almost constantly relive their trauma or all but dismiss it episodes later. Sometimes, shows even lean into stereotypes to give their villain characters basis for their behavior. I will admit that I don't know what it is like to write for TV, but despite enjoying aspects of shows like *Empire*, I find this truth troubling. These stories are the ones that receive critical acclaim, the stories of our pain and suffering. Yes, black people have suffered, been through hell and back, have built a nation on our backs, but I wonder why our pain and suffering is too often the only thing that moves the mainstream media? Of course, we have to tell these stories. They are important because black and brown history is American history and world history. We do feel pain and often experience differing levels of PTSD in relation to the pain inflicted on us. However, there are other stories that I think deserve to be told. With the success of *Black Panther* and *A Wrinkle in Time*, I can't help but notice the missing disabled bodies. I think we'd be great in Wakanda; we'd find and save our parents in alternative dimensions like Meg Murry does.

....

My hope is that we can reach a point in media representation where we can have quirky and weird characters, happy-go-lucky characters, annoying characters, and all-around unlikable characters who are black and brown without the assumption that these characters are representative of an entire community. Especially the unlikable characters. I want the chance to watch shows and movies without trying to figure out how long it will take until the characters of color with and without disabilities will die, will experience pointless trauma that does not advance the plot or will feed into dated stereotypes, or will find themselves without any true story line or character arc at all in favor of being another character's prop.

I want to see a wider range of black women and gender-nonconforming black people on TV and in movies. I want to see older black women, black women in the LGBTQ+ community, disabled black women, and fat black women not only in leading roles but also in love and happy. I want to know that these people and that these stories, including my own, matter enough to be seen in an inspiration porn–free light.

Black people with disabilities are all but invisible. We simply don't exist. The first and only time I can remember seeing a black physically disabled woman in a movie was Kerry Washington in *Fantastic Four* as Alicia Masters. This was the first portrayal of disability that I saw where the character didn't struggle with it, didn't treat it like it was ruining her life. This portrayal, while important, comes with its own set of issues. The biggest issue is that Kerry Washington is not actually physically disabled. Hollywood prefers to give disabled characters to able-bodied actors. Many people in the disability community refer to this as "crippling up": an able-bodied actor plays disabled, often to critical acclaim and the promise of awards, while a disabled actor isn't afforded the chance to tell the stories that he or she lives every single day.

Of course, I watched Kerry Washington every Thursday night on *Scandal* until its series finale and reveled in the fact that a black woman was the lead on a network television show that spanned the same time line as my journey to self-love (and predated it). Even with *Scandal*'s end, Thursday nights are dominated by Shonda Rhimes, a black woman who writes for and executive-produces that show and three others in what we Shondaland fans call TGIT (Thank God It's Thursday). What I love most about these Thursday nights is that each show—*For the People, Scandal, Grey's Anatomy*, and *How to Get Away with Murder*, the last of which was created by Peter Nowalk and executive-produced by Rhimes—all feature a diverse cast of characters that are given the room to be messy, broken, imperfect, and human in the way that all of us are in real life. They are given permission to deal with their trauma for as long as it takes. I will always be grateful for Shondaland for that, and it is in part why I want to write for TV (or even become a part of the Shondaland team one day).

As much as I love Shondaland and Shonda Rhimes, there is a bittersweet feeling in seeing the black people she's created in multidimensional roles on TV. I love it, yes, and I love them because the world is finally getting to see the people I have known all my life, the people who have always deserved to have their stories told. However, the lack of stories about disabled black people makes it hard to feel like I fit into the landscape of Shondaland and the haven it has become for me. My hope is that with Shondaland's new lifestyle website and what I'm sure will be more TV shows on the horizon via Shonda Rhimes's multiyear development deal with Netflix, there will be room for a black physically disabled girl like me.

The knowledge that you are an afterthought to someone stings in an all-encompassing way. Often when it comes to black disabled people and LGBTQ+ people, and especially any black person who inhabits those intersections, we come up as fodder for jokes or criticism in every community we inhabit, not just our black one. There are the ableist memes and jokes that are shared across all social media, and movements that are supposed to support all black lives tend to forget about disabled ones. This is part of the reason I have such a muddied history with the communities that I belong to, such as my black, disabled, and feminist communities. This muddied history with all my communities and my chosen identifiers makes me want to fight harder for more inclusion and respect. In the fight for representation, respect is an aspect that is not often discussed. My fight for representation in mainstream media is deeper than just thinking such representation would be cool. Don't get me wrong, it will be super cool, but my hope is also that proper representation will not only make room for a visibility that might shift the cultural view of disability, but also influence a change in tone with regard to respecting the lives and rights of disabled people, so that we can live in a world where we shouldn't be expected to apologize for the space we take up or the love we have for ourselves.

....

I still love the films I mentioned earlier: *Cinderella*, *Annie*, and *Mother Goose: A Rappin' and Rhymin' Special*. I love the TV shows I mentioned before, as well. Though I love those movies for the nostalgia they bring, for the years before I knew what disability would mean and how it would shape the way I live my life in our often-inaccessible world, I love TV shows for the possibility of a future that pushes further, that smashes past stereotypical ideas of marginalized characters and what they can be as a reflection of our real lives. Even before the surge of diverse faces and voices on our TV screens, when I was still idolizing white women in teen dramas and on reality shows, TV still felt like a glimpse into a future of happiness, a vehicle for hope. Now I think this even more. Despite my excitement for where the direction of media and popular culture is headed, I still feel like I'm living in a culture that finds disabled bodies too uncomfortable and broken to give us the characters, stories, and chances we rightfully deserve. As a black disabled woman who identifies as a feminist, I believe that my feminism stands on inclusion and the fact that what we have right now, despite how far we have come, is insufficient. We should be featured in romantic comedies, dramas, period films. We should be given the room to talk about disability in all its aspects, good and bad, without stories that end in death to the advantage of the able-bodied caretaker—as in the film *Me Before You* or in the simple wish to die as a result of disability, as in *Million Dollar Baby*. We should be featured in films and TV shows as characters who don't need their disabilities to be a central part of their story lines, because the truth is that able-bodied people think about our disabilities day-to-day more than we do. We adjust and adapt because of disability, not despite it. Sharing a more positive representation of disability can drown these negative narratives out.

I love TV and film so much, but I often find myself settling for scraps in terms of disability representation, even within the confines of the shows that I love. There are two shows that I think are shifting the conversation in a way I have never seen. First, NBC's *Superstore*, which I love with all my heart, features the character Garrett, a black man and wheelchair user played by Colton Dunn. The show hired a disabled woman who is also a wheelchair user to consult, though Dunn himself is not disabled. As much as I love the show, I can't in good faith ignore this fact; but for me, the consultant lessens a bit of the blow. I continue to see so much of myself in the character of Garrett even though I am a disabled black woman who does not use a wheelchair. I love his humor and quick wit and the fact that he is a character who engages in sexual activity without question, guilt, or fear, and a character whose personality is not his disability. His story lines and character arcs do not shy away from disability, but they are not his sole reason for existing in the Cloud Nine universe, and I love that. (Nonetheless, I know many activists who don't feel the same and wish the show had hired a disabled actor, believing that the consultant further proves that networks believe that we aren't good enough to be seen as we are in front of a camera but are good enough to be consulted.)

The second show that I loved—initially, that is—was ABC's *Speechless*. The show chronicles the life and experiences of a young boy named JJ who is nonverbal and has cerebral palsy. JJ, played by Micah Fowler, deals with his younger sister and brother, his passionate and sometimes overbearing mother, and his laid-back father. The show is great because JJ's family does not pity him or treat him as if he is a burden on their lives. However, Kenneth, JJ's aide, played by Cedric Yarbrough, is the only character of color on the show. Missing as well are disabled characters of color. In fact, most of JJ's interactions aside from those with Kenneth are with other white people. The show doesn't feature disabled people of color with speaking roles. I don't like to give up on shows, but I had to stop watching out of frustration. Often in the community, people of color are told to wait our turn or ignore our desires and specific challenges with regard to representation, as though the only concerns we should have are if white disabled people feel represented. I thought of this often when I was still watching *Speechless*, how it was a bittersweet bit of positive representation, how I had to go back to finding myself in white characters and celebrating that my white friends with disabilities had proper representation. I want *Speechless* to prosper; I hope it proves my worries wrong. If things change, I will go back to watching it and leave my disappointment in the past.

The reality is that even the shows we love can have their own sets of issues in their push for inclusion, but it is imperative that despite those hiccups we strive for a more inclusive future. We don't give effort the praise it deserves. Trying is an art even when you try and fail; every time you get up and keep going, when you stop dreaming and fight for what you want and what is necessary, that's when the real change and growth begins. This applies to everything, but especially to entertainment media. The only thing stopping most of us is a lack of access to the places necessary to see the dreams we fought for come to fruition. Now that we know the face of disability is still white, as well as the face of most entertainment TV and movies today, we can also recognize that change is necessary.

....

A few years ago, when I was still regularly using Tumblr—the place where my love of popular culture prospers without apology or pause even when I go weeks and months without posting—I made a post about representation saving lives. The post discussed celebrating black writers, scientists, artists, hosts, and filmmakers. As the saying goes, "You can't be what you can't see." I made the post in 2013, and it is still making the rounds because it is even more important now. I no longer wish to settle, and I will continue to fight for proper representation for disabled black people, because we are often the most invisible and underrepresented people both in the disability community and outside it.

I proudly wear each community label because each has given me people who understand me and support me in ways I never thought I deserved. People who love the same pop culture that I do and understand what it is like to not be seen and respected in the things that we love; these people keep me happy to be in the communities I claim on their worst days. As a whole, though, within each community structure and set of rules, I find that I am often expected to choose one over the other. I see this a lot in feminism; mainstream feminism is often white and able-bodied, often asking disabled people to forget their intersecting identities and focus on what all women need. (The feminist community and disabled community have this in common.) But thankfully, things seem finally to be shifting.

The disability community refuses to confront its racism, homophobia, and sexism. Instead, it insists that we focus on the bigger picture, as though the rest of our identities can be taken off to navigate each individual community. These communities are not the only ones that tend to forget about disabled people, especially those of us who are of color. The mainstream media does as well, even with a few recent exceptions.

I was once asked who I believe is left out of feminism and who I think can participate. The fact of the matter is that I am left out of feminism. Myself, and women and gender-nonconforming/nonbinary people who look like me, are left out. One of the main reasons for that is misogynoir. Misogynoir is defined as misogyny directed toward black women that uses both race and gender bias. This is most evident in the feminist heroes whom we celebrate today. The feminists who could *participate*. Women like Susan B. Anthony believed that the white woman deserved rights before the Negro, and Elizabeth Cady Stanton was a perpetrator of racist behavior, insinuating that her fight was only for white women of a certain income bracket. Our feminist history rarely praises the black women at the forefront. Black women like Ida B. Wells, Sojourner Truth, and Mary Frances Berry. These historical erasures are the reason that it is hard for some people to identify as feminists. The refusal to really confront the past wrongs and inequalities of feminism is the reason we lose the support of women who are feminists in every sense of the word but don't use the word because they are not properly represented. We have come a long way. There has been an effort to include more women and gender-nonconforming/nonbinary people in the community. However, even with every new step and stride, I can't help but think of the mirrors I once hated because I was my only representation.

I am still my only full representation. I have yet to see a black disabled woman in mainstream media. That is why I do this work— because I want more for myself and for the people who look like me and who question their worthiness because they don't know what it is like to be told they are beautiful and desirable. People who understand what it is like to love a culture and industries that don't know how to love you back, because they have not yet tried. The lack of representation of black disabled women fuels me when I feel like giving up, when I think that no one is listening, because if I can be the light for a black disabled girl, maybe she won't grow up hating mirrors. Maybe she'll grow up loving them and loving herself because she had someone who looked like her and who she saw loving herself. For me, being a black disabled woman and a feminist who loves popular culture wholeheartedly and has the ability to recognize its failings means that there will be hard days, there will be wars fought and battles hard won, and the reward will be giving black disabled girls the representation I never had. As well as selfishly longing for proof that I am beautiful and interesting enough to be featured in stories where we don't hate ourselves and don't die at the end of the shows and movies that I love.

My love for popular culture, for movies, for music, for television and cheesecake, matters as much to the making of me as my disability does. As human beings, we are never just one thing: one personality trait, one opinion, one set of likes and dislikes. We are multifaceted for a reason, because if we were all the same, the stories we tell would be very boring. So when I talk about popular culture, the bad has to come with the good. I cannot expect change without critique, and I wouldn't want it. My goal is not token representation, which is just the one character of color or disabled character who is there to try and quell criticisms; rather, my hope is for a multitude of disabled characters of color who reflect the ones I know in real life in all their complicated, honest, and unwavering beauty. So often, marginalized people do not even have the room to dislike the character who is supposed to be their piece of representation despite how terrible they are, because we almost always get only the one. I do not have all the answers and I cannot speak for every marginalized person, but I can tell you that I am tired of accepting scraps of representation. I want more, I want better. We all should.

YOU CAN'T CURE ME,
I PROMISE IT'S FINE

The first time that I was given an unsolicited cure for my disability, I was at the store in the CD section. I was maybe twelve and looking for what was likely an Avril Lavigne album because I was who I was and that's fine. I was searching and singing along to the song on the store speakers when a woman with a tight blond ponytail came up to me and said, "Oh, honey, I don't know what you have but I am praying for you, and the power of prayer fixes everything." She even added a thumbs-up before walking away, as though the exchange had been warranted or normal. I stood there in shock until she was out of my eyesight.

That exchange may come across as trivial to most people, but I still remember it as an important part of my being visible in public spaces. The gall of a woman to approach a twelve-year-old girl who only wanted a CD, simply to remind her just how different she was. As if she didn't know. As if it were not constantly on her mind already. Disability, in many ways, strips away the kinds of privacy and respect that should be understood but are instead ignored. I did not understand the effects of this until I was much older.

I would spend the years that followed this exchange receiving a further variety of unwarranted "solutions." The repeat offenders were and are as follows: essential oils, prayers, hypnosis, experimental surgeries, special creams, holy water, and yoga. Yoga is often regarded as the best option in these exhausting, lecture-like conversations. Out of all these things, I was offended most by the holy water. I believe in God, in heaven and hell, in spirits in and out of human bodies. I do so without apology and despite the cure narratives rampant throughout Christianity. My faith in God is deeper than what he could do for me, but it wasn't always. Our relationship was steeped in anger for a really long time. Yet I believed always, if not strongly, even though I pretended to be asleep more often than not when my family asked us all to get up and get ready for church.

Until the tail end of 2016, I did not come to God in thanks. I came only when tragedy struck and when he did not bring back my grandmother in 2009 and my uncle in 2014, I was convinced he did not care about my family, because if he had, he would have kept them alive. Admitting as much may open me up to criticism, but I want to be honest here. My relationship with God is now healthier than it has ever been, because before, I thought I deserved a cure, a miracle like those described in the Bible. *If God is a healer, why won't he heal me?* What I know now is that there is purpose behind his every action and the actions of his son, and I don't have to look to be healed in order for my own happiness and a life lived well.

For a while, though, I was resentful and contradictory, because my belief in him was real but my indignation at the body he put me in was more real. I felt I was being punished, and I did not know how to make up whatever I'd done to him so that he would not be angry with me anymore. That's the problem with some of the teachings of God in which disability and fear are concerned. We often hear of one (disability) as a catalyst or a punishment to the other (fear) or vice versa, thus leading to the idea of cure as a safety net from the wrath of God, meaning that if disability can be cured it could mean that we'd (the disabled) be spared from the wrath of God. As a child I often saw the late-night infomercials in which a preacher with a creepy mustache, a microphone, and the rapt attention of an audience in a megachurch sprinkled "holy" water on people with disabilities that caused them to limp, or on wheelchair users, or on deaf and blind people, before they'd stand up straight, tossing their canes or wheelchairs aside, limp-free. They did all this before yelling in praise of the water, the preacher, and the God who had healed them from whatever it was we consumers were to believe they had. They always talked in these infomercials about getting a second chance at life, as if every moment before that one had been no moment at all. The truth is that the infomercials were often the opposite of convincing, but I do not doubt that they made money in the same way that exploitive telethons seeking to raise money for genuinely good causes do—without the grasp on the harm false depictions cause. I am pretty sure these infomercials influenced my strong dislike of mustaches both then and now.

I hated those commercials because I knew that they were full of shit, yet a small part of me wished they weren't. I'd go to bed those nights asking God why he'd show me those infomercials to make me long for the lies they were selling if he knew they weren't real. In hindsight, the commercials were really low-budget and filled with actors and "preachers" who used the word of God for their own financial prosperity. These people are still in churches today. We do not believe in the same God; they believe instead in financial gain and harnessing an unsuspecting following for their own power. They were the kind of people who seemed like they wanted to be their own god of sorts.

I saw these infomercials about ten times and then, somehow, never again. I pictured God saying to me, "There, now you can stop praying away your disability and learn to love yourself." You, dear reader, can be certain that I did not listen. I can tell you, though, how many signs you can miss as a believer when you are so intent on being in your own way. If you are not a believer, just picture any time that you've worked to change your own mind about something. The moment that you do, you remember all those valid reasons people gave you to do it earlier, when you were not trying to hear them.

....

All the same, the habit already formed, I prayed for salvation from my body well into high school and long after the commercials stopped. I prayed knowing full well what God had already told me: "I won't cure you, because there is nothing to cure." I can be a very stubborn person who ignores the signs she doesn't like until she has no choice. I plugged my ears and heart like a child might, singing "la, la, la" so that I could not hear what I was supposed to. I was also a person who believed that God became fondly exasperated by my self-hatred and sent me another test around 2014. I was on Facebook minding my own business when a girl with whom I had gone to middle and high school posted a video of a preacher "healing" a girl with cerebral palsy. This girl knew me well, and she still didn't see the harm in her post. At this point, I didn't even like myself yet, but I was fuming with anger at the implication that disability could be healed when I knew otherwise, firsthand. I am not proud of this now, but I let her have it in the comments section. I told her she was the worst kind of person, one who used faith to push lies and make people feel less than whole. I reminded her of the damage that messages like hers did and why they were part of the reason disabled people often turned away from faith. I was not elegant in my wording. I did not know how to effectively articulate the feeling of otherness. But I tried my best.

She called my cell phone trying desperately to explain why she thought that everyone should be in awe of God's miracles, which was silly because it is possible to be in awe without the belief that the only true miracles deal with ridding people of disability. People want so badly to believe in the idea of perfection, of eternal happiness, and that desire is universal to most people, even those of us who know better. Still, it is packaged in the ideal of perfection as being able-bodied; thus the idea of perfection both on earth and in the afterlife is ableist in nature. Why can't my spirit be disabled? It would be disabled and cute, after all, so I don't see the problem. In the stories of the Bible, there are many people with disabilities who use them to help other people, thus fulfilling their purpose—however much I begrudge the idea that we have to perform and achieve in order for our lives to be valued. Instead of resenting God, I resent the idea that able-bodied people without chronic illness feel like experts in their opinions of disability when they are not, nor will they be. My Facebook friend and I eventually patched things up and ended our conversation all those years ago agreeing to disagree, even though sometimes it doesn't matter how long we take to tell people something; in the end they are going to believe what they want. I have not spoken to this person in years simply because our paths do not cross anymore, though I wish her well.

However, the exchange left me sour on the idea of good intentions, because they are often used to excuse toxic behaviors or ideals. People do not like to confront the ways in which they hurt people and the ways in which their beliefs perpetuate a culture that, in many ways, kills disabled people and gets away with it. Faith is often the first reason used to justify the killing of disabled people. I do not believe that this person wanted me dead, but she also did not understand what it was like to live in a society that literally, whether intentionally or not, justifies this kind of murder. I have read countless stories of parents and grandparents taking care of severely disabled family members until one day they decide to kill them. In fact, a recent study found that a disabled person is killed once a week by a family member or other caregiver. There are fifty-two weeks in a year, and a disabled human is murdered at least once every week, yet there is hardly any coverage or outrage about it. These stories are often framed in two ways: the killers just couldn't take it anymore, finding the caretaking too much for them to "deal" with, or they were just trying to set the disabled person free, because their faith told them that their "loved one" could be free of disability in death.

Often we see these stories explained away as sad yet understandable—and that is petrifying. For a person to kill another person who is just trying to live in cold blood and then to say the death is understandable happens only to those of us in marginalized communities, to the same disabled people who have cures pushed on them. And for what? So no nondisabled person will resist the urge to kill us? The ways in which we accept the deaths of human beings simply because of disability should frighten everyone, not just those of us who are disabled. The issue also lies in the coverage of these stories, because the journalists writing them love to focus on the killers' humanity, the way they shopped at the store, the kind things they once said about the victim, and the times when they let their frustrations out on Facebook. In the end, the reader is given all of the ammo to blame the victim for existing. This is why it is necessary to hire disabled writers in newsrooms and at publications, in order to avoid these flowery depictions and shift the conversation to the victim and the people left behind without them.

I will not say that I know what it is like to take care of a severely disabled person, but I can say that even when caretaking is hard, murder is not the answer. I worry most for the disabled kids with special education teachers who believe that God will rid us of disability but that we must "suffer" with it on earth first, and for those who view the disabled kids they teach as burdens while expecting to be considered heroes for teaching them. I have had some fantastic and terrible teachers as a black disabled girl, but I was never more insecure than when I was in the classrooms of the teachers who treated me as though my disability were a problem. Kids can sense that sort of thing and internalize that behavior. Sure, there is an extra set of challenges in teaching people with different levels of cognitive understanding, but I think there are teachers who simply should not be teaching because of the harm they put on these children.

As a disabled person, I resent the idea that we, in all forms and severities, should be punished for what is out of our control. After I posted on social media about the story of Aurelia Castillo, a young girl with cerebral palsy who was killed by her grandmother, a lot of the responses conveyed horror, but some made an effort to explain the stress of the situation. Even though those people were well-meaning, the effort to try and find justification for the murder of a young disabled girl does so much damage, because if your stress leads you to kill, the disabled person you are caring for does not deserve to be in your care. I have forgiven the Facebook friend who shared the healing video, but she was not my last run-in with people who preach the same things she was preaching that day. I have, however, since run across many people who believe that disability can be cured through prayer, that it is all disabled people can hope and want for. I did hope for and want a cure at one point in my life, but through effort and faith in the God I recognize, my goal changed from a cure to rights and wellness in this world—which all disabled people deserve without question.

....

Let's imagine for a moment that we live in the same universe as *The Flash* and I can switch between time lines. Let's say I try these cures suggested to me in the future, one in which I have forgotten all that I know now, a future that strips me of the little rights I have now and effectively makes me forget my worth. (History seems to be leaning that way, anyway, with these rollbacks of protections and rights for disabled people.) The essential-oil bottles look cute after I pay for them at the Disability Be Gone! mart (because of course there is a mart in this future; there is always a mart in the dystopia-like future movies). Denise, the bored cashier behind the counter, smiles genuinely when she sees me, as she and my niece are best friends.

"Another late night?" I ask, though we both know the answer. Denise is just working summer shifts before starting her sophomore year of college in the fall.

"You know all of this is bull, right?" Denise says as she bags the oils I have purchased.

"We'll see," I reply.

At the checkout counter I almost grab Anxiety Be Gone, but Denise shakes her head silently. Tonight's purchases are just for the physically visible disability anyway. Gardenias are my favorite flower, so I chose the oil that smells most like them.

"Thank you for shopping at Disability Be Gone! May all your problems melt away." Denise rolls her eyes at her own words and comes from behind the counter to give me a hug. I promise her that the three of us will go to lunch before she and my niece leave for school again.

After telling Denise to have a nice night, I head home and set everything up. The oils smell great, truly, but they do nothing, and I worry that I bought the wrong ones. I am tasked with writing about the oils as cures, and a part of me is sad that I have to be the one to write a takedown of the gardenia oils, but the people need to know. Upon my return to Disability Be Gone! mart, I learn that the store is closed and that I must come back the following day. I return only for the prayers that were promised at the bottom of the receipt in place of monetary compensation in the event that the oil didn't work. I decide then that I can't write another takedown if it's unsuccessful, because sometimes the disappointment weighs on your soul. Denise is there only to squeeze my hands before saying "I told you so" as fondly as she can muster and handing me a voucher that's valid only in the church down the street.

I leave my car at the mart and decide to walk the small distance (I can drive in this future with the help of modifications). I decide to walk, though, because there are still Fitbits in this future and I have a step goal to reach. When I enter the church, I touch every mahogany-stained pew, stopping at the fourth pew on the left side to sit and pray. The left is my strongest side and four is my favorite number, so when I sit in this pew I feel at home. This is the pew I sit in every Sunday but the pastor never prays over me in the hopes that our God will rid me of my cerebral palsy. He's said he doesn't buy into the idea that God gave me this body just to cure me of it, but who knows what will happen when I pray for it myself?

The teenage version of me is anxious at the idea of saying these words again, anxious about the way they might change something, even if she and I are not sure what. They feel familiar to our tongue, but we try not to think much of it. I remind her that we are doing this because we have forgotten what we know; maybe prayer will help us find it. There is no time frame on prayer—no believer can pinpoint when or if a prayer can be answered—but I do it anyway. God really takes the "he may not come when you want him" thing seriously. I sit in the church at my pew praying for an hour for this cure, because when I pray for other things I feel good—or rather, I know that I will eventually. This does not feel good, nothing that you have to force ever does, but I press on. You remember what happened the first time, right? In the other time line, the fond exasperation and the waiting for realization? Well, the same thing has happened in this future time line, too. Since I was already at the church, I inquired about the holy water that I saw as my other self, but the church gift shop was all out and they apparently frown on the idea of those in-fomercials, too, so I don't know why they were selling it in the first place. But I digress. Capitalism is still a thing.

After a few days of self-reflection and a much-needed break—because trying to cure yourself takes a lot out of anyone—I make up my mind to try hypnosis next. I decide to work with a black woman named Jackie because she tempers my expectations before our sessions begin. Sometimes you need people who will kindly tell you that you're expecting more than you are going to get. We go out for pizza and see movies together. Jackie becomes my friend when she isn't supposed to, but I don't mind; I pay her as if she isn't. Jackie is great; she tells me all about her past selves so I can be prepared to meet mine, and when I do, they are all disabled, too. My favorite, Anna-belle, tried cures for her physical disabilities, too, but gave up when she became tired of the wear and tear on her body. I understand her best, and Jackie believes that is the point. Hypnosis for my future self is fun and cute in theory, but the lack of control messes with our equilibrium. My past selves are okay with their bodies with each visit and new self, and when we come to, we are still very much disabled.

After hypnosis, there are those suggestions of creams and surgeries. Here in this future, where I have forgotten what I know and
hold steadfast to the idea that I must work to rid my body of disability, I try the surgery first. Unlike the other time line, in which things
go well, in this one I am Jessica Alba in *Awake*; once the doctors realize the lawsuit on their hands, they sew me back up and apologize
profusely, but this isn't the kind of thing apologies can fix. (We are
still in court proceedings for that, so I can't say much more.) No one
ever told me what the names and colors of the special healing creams
were supposed to be, but we could consider it a scavenger hunt. I
could scour this future time line looking for clues on street corners
and in secret hidden passageways, but that feels like too much work,
so I don't. To be fair, in both time lines, the real and imagined, I've
searched high and low to find only cocoa butter sticks and lotion,
which would work better on fading my scars if I used them regularly.
Even after I shower and lather it in, my body does not transform, my
fingers do not magically straighten, nor does my hip or my spine.
The pain is still there when it wants to be. The pain is one of the
factors of disability that I cannot control. All I can do is try my best
to take back the narrative about what living with disabilities is like.

....

In each and every time line, the actual and fictitious, the cures suggested to me never work, but the problem is not theirs or mine. The
problem and the solution lie in the actions of those handing out the
suggestions in the first place, both the people who mean well and
the ones who do not. Disability is not monolithic, and because that
is the truth I can say with certainty that some disabled people live in
a world of pain and could use pain relievers to live a better quality
of life—a life that they deserve to live. I will not behave as though

disability is painless and that medicine isn't more often than not necessary to keep us going, to keep us alive. Still, pain should not be the center of our narratives, a reason to dismiss everything else that matters about us; if we do so, we will cease to be people at all. I have lost count of the number of times holistic medicines have been suggested to me simply because the person suggesting them read some article that was a takedown of modern medicine in favor of a "natural" approach to my wellness. I am all for holistic medicine for other people, I understand the acupuncture for chronic migraines, but I want to be real: it's not curing my cerebral palsy. The case against many medicines in the fight for wellness is ableist in nature. But that's a whole different story.

The problem is also not one of a relief from pain but rather the idea that without the proper qualifications or relationship some people feel it is okay to offer up their ideas or solutions to a pain that is not theirs. Those solutions can sometimes do more harm than anything else. However, because disability is not monolithic and we should be seen as human beings with our own autonomy, disabled people deserve the ability to live our everyday lives without the reminder that the world is not comfortable with the way we look, without having to navigate the world or the belief that we should want to change it and accept any and all suggestions from complete strangers. When I was a kid, I heard a lot about putting bass in your voice, the confidence to believe what you are saying, and I think that is what happens when people believe enough in what they are saying to think it is helpful instead of injurious. One of the first things I learned about my life after the realization and effort it took to want to live it is that just by existing, without causing physical or verbal harm to anyone else, many of us will make people angry, upset, or uncomfortable. They will say that we cost too much, take up too much space, and demand too many human rights, that our existence is tainting some "pure" idea of what a body should be. Their discomfort cannot continue to be our problem. Instead, it has to be the problem of everyone else. When we see this ableist discrimination, we cannot always put ourselves in harm's way simply to make a point. It is not as if we are expecting anyone to take bullets for us, but I think that when injustices occur and thus are used to create harmful societal norms, a person in a privileged position can and should say something to curb further injustices. At the end of the day, disabled people are just being, existing, loving, and hating, and we have that right.

Our history behind the urgency for cures is not solely about the discomfort in the way our bodies look and function but also about control and the desire to harness that control into a believed tangibility. In the movie *Everything, Everything* we see this play out clearly. The protagonist, Maddy (Amandla Stenberg), is eighteen and has severe combined immunodeficiency (SCID). Maddy is susceptible to infections, so her mother, Pauline (Anika Noni Rose), keeps her in their home and bans her from ever going outside. As in many teen movies and romantic comedies, Maddy meets a boy. This boy is named Olly (Nick Robinson), and before they know it, they've fallen in love through text messages and dreams of the world at large. Olly increases Maddy's desire to see the world outside her home—and to do so with him. In all fairness, I think the movie is cute; the actors have chemistry and Maddy's outfit choices are A+ and in line with my own personal sense of fashion. I understand her longing for more, desiring to travel and see the world, and, in the clichéd way, discovering herself along the way. I love a good romantic comedy or drama, a story of two people falling in love. The issue for me with this movie, which was based on the book by the incredibly talented Nicola Yoon, is that by the story's end we learn that Pauline has pretended that Maddy had SCID to keep her safe after she lost her husband and other child years prior.

I know what you're thinking. "What's wrong with that? Now Maddy can go and explore the world with Olly and we can believe in a happily-ever-after." I love a happy ending as much as the next romantic-movie lover, but the important question is for whom that the happy ending is truly intended. Not for the people in real life with SCID, who are essentially being told that a life inside is no life at all.

I am disabled and I tried all those cures—some in real life and some in an imagined time line—and they didn't work and weren't supposed to. I am still happy without them. I am still living my life well: my life and the lives of other actually disabled people are filled with adventure. These words are an adventure; so are the panels and speeches we are on and do, that take place indoors. If adventure is the mark of a life well lived, then many of us are right on track without the inherent ableism and hatred that comes with the idea that we must desire to be rid of parts of ourselves to be whole.

What I often liken an invasion of privacy to is parenting. I have kids in the *Sims 4* game. Some toddlers I send to day care when their Sim parent doesn't have work, and I have some teenagers who do their homework but stay out past curfew, but I am still not qualified to give out advice about parenting, because I am not a real parent. If you are not disabled and if you are not being asked for your advice, don't force it on a disabled person. We cannot all be experts at everything, so we can't just expect that our unsolicited advice is valuable or necessary, when in reality, it is often about ego and insisting that we must put our own comfort above someone else's. Parents get testy when you try to tell them how to rear their children, and rightfully so: they have them 24/7 and we do not. They deserve their privacy and we deserve ours. Still, no one is perfect, and sometimes you get the urge to say something when a kid is crying in the store or kicking the back of your airplane seat, like Angelica in *The Rugrats Movie*, or to "help" a disabled person because you have decided that what she is doing isn't working or seems unsafe. Notice how in most cases we stop ourselves? Because we know our lanes and we stay in them, because there is no traffic. No one walks up to another person that he does not know to tell her that she is putting items in her grocery store cart wrong or that she is trying clothes on the wrong way, and that restraint is likely present to keep the situation from escalating into possible violence. Well, in that same vein, disabled people do not need strangers or people we do know telling us how we should try to fix or change our bodies when we never said we had a problem with our bodies in the first place. As with parents who parent, and with people shopping and trying on clothes, those same people eager to "encourage" should assume that if we aren't causing ourselves or anyone else harm, there is no need to step in and offer unsolicited advice.

When Stephen Hawking passed away in 2018, I wrote about the ways fans and writers used ableist language and photos in what they believed were tributes to one of the greatest intellectuals in history. They diminished and belittled who he was in his entirety. They turned his disability into his sole attribute just to imply how free he was from it. I received piled-on hate because I pushed back against the idea that he was now "free" of his wheelchair and disability. If he was able to change the world while here on earth with his disability and wheelchair, why strip him of it just because he had passed? Why behave as though his disability were a hindrance to his intelligence and breakthroughs instead of an aide? The thought process behind such reasoning is dishonest at best. It further proves the point that many people are uncomfortable with disability be-

cause they can't and don't want to understand it. To try and understand it is to be okay enough with yourself in every stage of growth
and being so that you do not see your body as damaged. To try and
understand is to recognize humanity in what you yourself may not
be able to explain without having to see yourself as disabled to do
so. Having to remind people to care just because something might
involve them later is exhausting after a while. We should care for
people on the basis of empathy, respect, and kindness.

The careless words and tributes to Dr. Hawking felt like slaps in
the face to me. That is why I said yes to writing the piece for *Teen
Vogue* in the first place, because I was upset with some of the ways
he was being memorialized by able-bodied people. In response to
my piece, the able-bodied people who complained about it used
Dr. Hawking's perceived pain as a counterpoint to my piece. They
thought they could use it as a way to silence my credibility, and in
some ways, his. People couldn't see the irony: they were turning the
pain of a disabled person into his only trait to prove that he needed
to be free of disability. They didn't understand the need for breakthroughs in medicine that would have allowed his pain to subside
without curing ALS. They were projecting a pain onto Stephen
Hawking that he did not publicly express. He did make it known,
however, that he did not hate his disability, so it was frustrating that,
in his death, his life became solely about his suffering and not his
lifechanging breakthroughs. What was even funnier was that my
loudest detractors were people who had never experienced disability
of their own, but that's usually how it goes, and those ideals are influenced by a culture that focuses only on the pain and hardship of
disability because it is what is packaged and sold. Our joy is far from
the assembly line.

When we strip people of parts of who they are like this, we are effectively ignoring the people with those parts who are alive, telling them they should embrace the idea of death as freedom. Stephen did not believe in the afterlife, but I believe that when he was here on earth his wheelchair and technology were his freedom in that they allowed him to continue living his life the way he saw fit. He once said that without his disability and the technology he used as a result, he would have been doing research and paperwork that he would not have wanted to do in the first place. In the midst of the ableist language surrounding his death, there were also pictures of Stephen standing and staring at the stars with his chair in the distance behind him, which also felt gross because his chair was not keeping him from viewing the stars. It was not a prison.

....

In order for real change to occur, to end the detrimental cure narratives, there is language that needs changing. The use of "suffering from" needs to go first. When you view actual people from the context of their suffering, you are willfully ignoring their humanity. And often, the "suffering from" language is presumed, because the person writing it assumes that those of us with a disability spend every moment of every day suffering simply because we are disabled. A gentle spoiler: we do not. With language as a universal connection, we need to rid our vocabularies of words like "handicap," "retard," and "special needs," because in addition to sugarcoating disability to make it more palatable for people without it, these words and phrases infantilize disability and lead nondisabled people to believe the disabled are children just hoping for a cure to the common cold—as though disability is not rich in its intricacies and diversity, as though we live wanting nothing else than to be free of it. The real force behind cures is infantilization, and the infantilization of disabled people is a molder of the societal view of disability. This sentiment is true even for the people who seem to be disgusted by us. They consider us a stain on the fabric of society because we require care that is coming out of their "taxes." (I use quotes because many of these people barely pay their taxes, but logic isn't their strongest point.) Then there are the people who think that a cure will save us—or simply make us more convenient and less of an eyesore. I know this view sounds like an exaggeration, but I have run into people like this, and I mention them now only to showcase how deep their hatred actually is.

A lot of the desire for cures comes out of the superiority complex that strangers have (strangers such as those who give unsolicited advice, for example). We live in and navigate a world that upholds that complex in design, opportunity, function, and more. Those of us who live outside able-bodied-ness are forced to adapt, viewed as outliers and problems that need to be fixed. We are not problems. We are people who deserve the same rights to life, liberty, and the pursuit of happiness as everyone else. The fight for change is not ours alone. We need to end the constant cure narratives ingrained and championed within our culture. We need to end the "just kidding, you were never sick" narratives, the "death means freedom from disability" narratives, and the idea that if the body is not 100 percent able all the time, it is to be pitied and dismissed while simultaneously being molded into something it cannot ever be. Also, stop the "advice," people. It's not as good or as helpful as one might believe it to be. Odds are that whatever suggestions someone may have for disabled people to try, we have already tried it or determined that we did not need to, and it is not as if we need to change ourselves to fit societal standards. The standards need to change to fit us.

Once we do away with cure narratives and the misconception that they are disabled people's every waking thought, we can move

on to the things that disabled people actually *need* and *deserve*.
For starters: respect. It is so interesting how we talk about inclusion
and diversity and the respect of telling those stories but conveniently
forget the respect where disabled people are concerned. This lack of
respect isn't just for representation in mainstream media. It is a lack
of respect for disabled people in everyday life, and respect is much
more important than pity.

We also need steady housing, a place to live. More than 40 percent of America's homeless population includes people with disabilities, and that is just the percentage of the people who have reported
having a disability. Cures do not matter when you're just trying to find
shelter and a roof to sleep under at night and in life. We need a source
of stable income. Contrary to popular belief, social security income
(SSI) payments keep their recipients just above the poverty line with
no real way to save, making it an effort to get off the program without
a relative miracle. SSI is a rigid system that punishes people who can
work the odd job from time to time with a rule saying that saving
anything over two thousand dollars is grounds to be kicked out of the
program. This doesn't make it easy to survive in a world where two
thousand dollars is given the same weight as ten thousand dollars,
in a program where most people receive around seven hundred dollars max a month. People in the program who could save exactly two
thousand dollars are rare, and they likely have other members of their
family to think about when factoring in their income.

Health care and the threats to Medicaid by the Trump administration are a threat to our livelihoods and the protection of our
ability to receive the necessary medical care. We lack accessibility to
a lot of public spaces and thus the ability to do things like vote, run
for office, protest injustices in person, and navigate the world. The
idea of a catchall cure seems so silly now, doesn't it?

We have much more important things to fight for, more work to be done. The better question is not "How can we cure disability?" but "Why can't we just accept people for who they are?" If you ask me, that's less work and more fun. Let's stop assuming we understand or know how someone lives and exists in the world based on their body type. Let's stop assuming we know what is best for other people, because you end up looking a mess when you try and tell strangers how they should live their lives and feel about themselves. I promise you, I don't need your cures or poorly thought-out pieces of advice, but I'll take free designer clothes, cheesecake, and a first-class plane ticket. I want what many people do: the room to just be in the world buying music and enjoying myself. Oh, and I went to a yoga class once. I got really sweaty and the music was great, but my body hated it.

FREEDOM OF A PONYTAIL

I was twenty-four years old when I could finally put my hair into a ponytail. This may seem trivial, but it matters, especially when you have spent most of your life keenly aware of all the things you can't do. The knowledge of the things you can't do comes from trial and error, from a society built without your body in mind. My cerebral palsy shapes not only how I view the world but also how I navigate through it, and because cerebral palsy affects the right side of my body, the most seemingly simple tasks are hard for me. Tasks like clasping pants, opening bottles, zipping jackets, carrying more than one thing at a time, and balancing myself, to name a few. And so, putting my shoulder-length hair into a ponytail by myself had always been out of reach—until four years ago.

I didn't feel embarrassed about needing help with my hair until high school. I never saw it as a big deal. My mom helped me, and I went about my way believing that everyone had help from a mom or parent in some way, that all people were still trying to figure out how to take care of themselves while they figured out who they were and who they wanted to be. When the embarrassment came, it did for the standard reasons it often does: with age and puberty come insecurities, and though I developed early and began having my period in middle school, my insecurities only grew when I hit the high school hallways. I'd watch enviously as my classmates put their hair up before gym class. My eyes would follow them as they walked through the halls without limps, ponytails bouncing along happily as their bearers made their way to their boyfriends' lockers, as they navigated the desire of other boys and, again, the world of high school and the certain attractiveness beyond its halls.

My identical twin sister, Leah, was one of those girls. She doesn't have cerebral palsy, and she can put her hair up without even thinking about it. She isn't just good at a ponytail, though; if I need braids, twists, or just a hair look for a night out, I can turn to her to make me extra cute. She is also much more proficient at makeup than I am, and she drives. Back in high school, I wanted to be her. I wanted a body with completely functioning hands and feet, a body without a right leg that was shorter than the left. I wanted to wake up glad that I had woken up. I gave validity to every stereotypical idea that I, a disabled woman, hated my body, that I should hate it because there was no other choice. Whenever the idea of disability was brought up in social circles or on TV, it was done in jest or disgust. I was always the exception, and I reveled in it. I didn't want to resent God for giving me crooked lips and fingers, aching knees and hips, but I did.

Even though Leah or my mom would help me every morning without complaint, having to wait until they were done getting ready and then ask them to fix my hair really bothered me. At fourteen and sixteen, seventeen and eighteen, I still had to depend on someone else to do something that everyone around me could do alone; it was an easy disappointment to internalize. I was striving for a kind of independence I knew I might never have. I would go to school and my friends would say, "Oh, you put your hair up. It looks really cute," but I knew that I hadn't done it, my mother or my sister had done it for me. A small smile and a nod kept me from telling the truth. In gym class, after I changed my clothes, my hair would fly free from my perfectly coiffed ponytails. I knew that if I took them out, I could not put them back in, so I tried my best to tame them once more with my fingers, tucking the stray hairs behind my ears, but they never looked as good as they did before. I blamed myself and what I believed to be my incompetence, because it felt like I was the only girl in the world with this problem. The ability to put my hair into a ponytail was just another thing that I couldn't do, regardless of how hard I wished for it at night. I resigned myself to being stuck until some outside force changed or bent the odds in my favor. I was Danielle Harris as Hayley Wheaton in the TV movie *Wish Upon a Star*, just wishing for what I believed was better and more popular. At that age, I believed wishes to be cures and allowed myself to be disappointed when they didn't come true, because life was never like the movies, no matter how overused the phrase may be. I imagined boys thinking, *She can't even put her hair up. Why would I go out with her?* Nevertheless, I didn't really work on my ponytail dream in high school. My schedule was already full. I was too busy honing my sarcasm and low self-esteem. Being one of the girls with the long, swinging hair just seemed out of reach, like a mission destined to fail. And in truth, my defeatist attitude kept me from achieving so much in those years.

Leaving high school and entering college introduced a whole new set of challenges. In college, without my mom or my sister to help me, I tried every trick imaginable to put my hair up. For a while, I used a claw. I had a black one and a brown one. But the claw didn't give me a ponytail; it just pulled all my hair up and triggered some of my worst chronic headaches when I wore it too long. That, and even when I could clamp one side of my hair and stuff the other inside the claw, it would not always stay that way. The sloppiness of it all reminded me too much of having to make do after gym class years before. The claw was quickly followed by a bejeweled tuck comb, which never worked, either. I always ended up sending the comb skittering across the room because it could not find purchase in my hair. I shouldn't have been as surprised as I was, considering that out of the three that I bought, there were exactly zero people on the packaging with hair that looked like mine. I was used to being in majority-white spaces by that time, but I was not used to the loss of access to people like my sister and mother, who understood the struggle of taking care of my hair. When it was too much to manage and when a relaxer was necessary, I took the bus home on weekends to Buffalo, where my mother would pick me up and take me to my beautician, Ann, on Saturday before taking the bus back on Sunday. (Ann still works her magic on my hair today, keeping it manageable enough to put in a ponytail when I please.)

When I desperately needed for my hair to be swept up, I would ask my roommates or hallmates to help me, and they were happy to do it, but I was the only black person in my friend group. When we spent weekends at Leigh's family cottage, getting my hair wet, especially after a relaxer, was a big concern of mine, and so I asked Leigh or her sister, Melissa, when I had to. When I did not, if my hair got wet, it got wet. I knew that my hair was very different from that of my friends. My hair was thick, and it took a lot of time and patience to get it to cooperate. They weren't sure how to approach it, and I never expected them to be. I was thankful to them for even trying, but it pointed out the glaring differences between us, so I tried not to ask very often. I didn't like the idea of making them uncomfortable or doing anything that may have made them regret getting to know me. Instead, I used the claw or the comb, or I wore my hair down.

Asking for help made me feel like an outsider, like the younger me watching those girls with the perfect hair. For a lot of disabled people, the offer for help is given without our explicit consent, and it feels infantilizing, especially when we don't ask for it. We often are reduced to obstacles that able-bodied people must find a way around. Oftentimes, the help is born out of the idea that we are inconveniences more than anything else. My words here are harsh, but this has been my experience in the case of strangers asking me if I need help and becoming indignant when I politely decline. Disabled people are not "good deed for the day" tickets. We are human beings with autonomy first, and that is how we should be treated. If we say we're good, trust us, we don't always need saving.

The fear of infantilization and the anger of others is what makes me weary and ashamed when I know I need help, because of the automatic belief that I need help by society at large. I never want to become a burden to someone else or a group of people. There is the saying about "pulling your own weight," and I tend to overcompensate and overwork my body just to keep up. It is harmful both physically and emotionally, but it is a bad habit that I have yet to unlearn. I am still ashamed when my body needs a break but I feel like I don't. I just want the ability to keep up, but what I need is to recognize it isn't possible and to be kinder to myself. I hope I get there. The shame also comes from the necessity for help with even small things, from the frustration that my body allows me less independence sometimes. My friends and family are great about it, though: they call me out for not just asking them for help, because they don't help me out of pity for my disabled body, but because they know that whatever they can do to help make something faster or easier for me will help us all in the long run (at least, where time is concerned). I have been this way for as long as I can remember. I have never allowed myself the space to be okay with how much I have to ask for help. I liken it to the responsibility of chores as a child: you don't want to do it but you have to, and a part of me still feels like asking for help makes me less of an adult even though I know this is not true. In having the right people in my life, I seldom have to worry about being a burden, and my friends happily remind me that my disability is a part of me, yes, but it doesn't make them think less of me or my abilities to be the friend they deserve.

....

I graduated from college in 2013, and while I was living back at home and looking for a job like most college grads with the unrealistic expectation of instant employment, I had a lot of free time. I made a list of all the things I could and couldn't do: I couldn't walk for long periods without leg and hip pain, I couldn't ride a bike, and I was paralyzed with fear at the idea of running, because to run is to inevitably fall, and, the embarrassment of falling aside, I was and am afraid of getting hurt. As a child, I never had that fear, even after every surgery, but in high school, the fear of running and getting hurt crept in. I couldn't skip, or swim, or sing ever, or dance well enough to command a dance floor and an excited crowd. I couldn't keep my shoes tied tight for long. You get the picture, don't you?

In hindsight, the list was very self-deprecating and self-pitying. Part of me really wrote it only just to break my own heart and take a shot at myself because it was easy. What I know now is that it is very easy to get comfortable in your defeat. Still, after looking at the list, I knew that there were things that would require more time and different settings. I knew I couldn't teach myself to swim in April, regain full motor usage in my right hand in May, or ride a bike in June; tamping down my expectations was necessary. I decided I was going to learn how to do a ponytail on my own, no matter what anyone thought, myself included, or how long it might take.

I tried YouTube tutorials because I am a visual learner. *Search: How do I put my hair into a ponytail using one hand?* There are lots of videos on this topic, mostly made by amputees. But the videos showed only white women with hair long enough to position between their shoulder and chin to keep it in place, hair long enough to put between doorframes and dangle behind chairs. The search results are also indicative of the overall whiteness in representation for the disability community, which lends itself to an even bigger problem. I am certain that there were other women who look like me searching for the same thing who found possible solutions, but I never saw them.

Search: One-handed ponytail with short hair. The results were more of the same, until I found a video showing a technique I thought might actually work. It featured a special hair tie called the 1-Up—basically an elastic string with a toggle. My aunt Renee made me one, and I followed the video's instructions. The hope was that my nondominant right hand would be able to help my stronger left hand and create this seemingly easy ponytail. I envisioned a new morning routine where I would stand beside my sister while she did her hair and I did my own. I imagined walking into a dressing room at the mall and trying on clothes with the ease and nonchalance of a girl who could confidently put her hair back up when she was done. I imagined leaving my house in my ponytail to find that someone thought I was cute when his eyes landed on me with a curiosity that had nothing to do with my limping leg.

I was proud of a ponytail I hadn't successfully made and imagining a life made for the movies—until reality crept in. I needed to pull the string with my right hand while my left hand held down the toggle, and my right hand wasn't strong enough. *I* wasn't strong enough.

After two weeks, I had to give up on the 1-Up. I am admittedly very hard on myself. I pick the smallest things apart and hold on to them because I get angry at myself when I don't know how to do something, and this was no different. I fell back into my routine of insults and frustrations, of self-inflicted pain and blame.

I thought not being able to put my hair up made me a failure. I let it deter and change me; I added it to a list of reasons I hated myself. I had and still have this urgency for normalcy—whatever that may be. There is still so much left for me to unlearn. Right now, though, I am your problematic fave who still yearns for acceptance from people who may never accept her at all. I am no longer ashamed of my body, but I do long for conventional attractiveness, and the quest for an unassisted ponytail felt like my way in.

Search: What's wrong with me? Why can't I do this simple thing? Why is this my life? Will there ever come a time when I do not need to ask my sister to put my hair up once she is finished with her own?

Doing my own ponytail was part of a dream of self-sufficiency, a chance to believe that I was someone worth something. If I could do that, I could achieve other things. I felt desperate to be able to do this. It was one of the first times I did not give up on myself even in the midst of all my self-loathing at my first failed attempt. I began practicing in secret, paying close attention to the ways that people in my life did theirs. As soon as my mother and my sister left for work, I would park myself in front of the mirror, brush in hand, and try to put my hair up all day. I practiced for weeks in the same chair, in front of the same mirror, with tear-stained cheeks for every failed attempt, but I kept going, I kept trying; and looking back, I can see that it was a monumental decision, because it was so different from who I was otherwise at the time. The choice to get up and dust myself off to try again was a surprising one, and I wouldn't realize its importance until long after the fact.

On a Wednesday in April 2016, in the middle of a rainstorm, after trying for three weeks, I finally did it. I gathered as much hair as I could in my left hand and put the elastic around it, then put the low ponytail into my right hand and used my left hand to twist the elastic around and tighten it. The resulting ponytail wasn't perfect, but I cried like I'd won a Pulitzer. I walked over to the cabinet in my kitchen, the one that holds the pictures of my uncle who passed away in 2014 and my grandmother who passed away in 2009, to show them what I'd done. I like to think that they were cheering me on. If anyone could understand my desire for some semblance of independence, it would be them. When they were alive, we talked about it often, about my desire to do and be more. In my heart, they always saw my potential long before I ever saw it. That is the way it seems to work: when we are looking for the most honest answers about who we have the potential to be, we can often look to the people closest to us.

I took the time to celebrate myself after the first ponytail was made. I cried tears of joy to the mirror and again that night when I was alone in the dark of my room. Two months later, I would write about ponytails in the online newsletter Lenny Letter to extend the celebration. These new sloppy ponytails gave me a taste of the self-sufficiency I longed for. They were a starting point to more discovery, more achievements both personal and professional. They were my promise of more to come, a promise to keep working at them until they were the best that they could be. I found myself wondering back to that list of things I couldn't do and imagining a world, a version of myself, who could. Now that I was able to do this one thing, the others didn't seem so impossible.

Reflecting on my ponytails four years after the fact, I see that my technique is the same. Except now, once the ponytail is in, I take my thumb and index finger and place them under the ponytail holder and push it closer to my head to make sure that the ponytail itself is as tight and close to my head as possible. My ponytails are not as sloppy as the very first one, because I have been practicing, but they are messy. Messy, yes—not the kind of cute, messy buns you see on Instagram, but the kind of messy that one could learn to live with. My ponytails, three years in, are still my favorite expression of independence. They have allowed me to admit that I want to try braids, twists, curls, and smooth and tight ponytails. I can use my hair as another expression of creativity and as a window into who I am. As I said, ponytails are not as trivial as we sometimes make them out to be. For example, I have been really into throwing hats over them, your standard baseball-style hats with a cute flower design; tying a high ponytail, which requires assistance; forming a bun that I tuck in and then fluff out so that it looks more effortless or just pulling it back as I lounge around my house writing, to keep it out of my face. As a teenager, I was desperate to express femininity because I believed femininity worked in tandem with desirability. I know now that isn't always the case, because I have the ability to look attractive with my hair bone straight or in curls. That, and women don't have to perform femininity to be attractive, because it is a very subjective choice, attractiveness. Still, it is something else entirely to be able to pull my hair back for the right outfit, to pop on some earrings and know my own worth regardless of whether any romantic interest might. I feel free, at best free of my own negative expectations. In my ponytails I feel like I can fly. Sure, it is a very cheesy analogy and feeling, but it is the truth. I may never be as desirable as those high school girls and I may never reach the level of femininity that I once longed for all those years ago, but this feels good for me.

....

I am also currently trying to learn the art of makeup. I am decent with lipstick and a massive fan of CoverGirl lip stains and Fenty Beauty matte lipsticks. Long before I felt beautiful without lipstick, I felt ugly but invincible with it. I love red lipsticks despite not being a big fan of the color in most other capacities, but I am also branching out into browns, purples, pinks, blues, and soon—when I find the courage—black. When I pop on a lipstick I feel so good, the closest to sexy I will ever be. The love for lipsticks began in high school, tied to desirability but also personality. The hot girls in all my favorite movies wore red lipstick, and all the guys and some girls wanted to be with them or be their friends. I wouldn't allow myself to wear the lipsticks I loved until college. I bought them in high school but never wore them, because I thought they had to be earned. As I grew older, I stopped treating lipstick like a thing I didn't deserve, couldn't obtain, like beauty. Lipstick became a reward. If I did great on a test or did something kind for a friend, I would go home and put it on, relishing the fact that I had earned it. From that point on, I would wear lipstick after I earned it. I would wear it at college house parties and after finals, at college graduation and after every essay acceptance. I've gotten better at the application of lipstick, a skill that came with practice and patience that I didn't know I possessed. Lipstick is the only thing that I can apply without help, and it feels good to still love it so much all these years later, to grow with it in this way.

The next aspect of makeup that I am working on is eye shadow. Right now, we—my eyelids and I—are in the early stages and using the cheap stuff to practice with. We are admittedly terrible at blend-ing, but practice makes perfect—or, at least, that is what I say to the mirror before we begin. I roam the aisles of Walmart in awe because there are so many options. There are warm colors that remind me of fall: browns, deep orange, white, off-white, and the like. We also have bright blues and dark greens, the colors infused with so much glitter it will end up everywhere. I imagine them all on my eyelids, with the right outfit and the right attitude—there is nothing that a head-to-toe look cannot do. I have been told I have great eyelids for all types of eye shadow, whatever that means. Part of me believes I need the expensive brushes, as though they will elevate me in the craft quicker. The reality is, I am a little too overconfident. After buying one blending brush, I am still not sure how to properly use it, but I'm confident that I'm not using it correctly. Once I tire of the brushes that I have no idea how to use, I am going to try blending with my fingers, because I hear it's easier. I have been using a purple CoverGirl palette and an LA Colors palette but I am hoping to try a Wet n Wild palette because its packaging shows what color should go where. I think I could benefit from the clear instructions.

After eye shadow, I want to learn how to highlight. I have been told that there are highlight sticks, so those are the ones that I will gravitate toward. The tricky thing about highlight is when it is streaky. As a newbie in all of this, I do not want to look like I put a glittering streak down the sides of my cheeks because I didn't blend it in properly. To avoid this, I watch a lot of beauty and makeup tutorials on YouTube but do not attempt to do anything with them, as we—my eyelids and I—are not at that stage in the learning process yet. Learning how to fill in my eyebrows is a must as well, because they are so light they are almost nonexistent. I'd like to model my dream eyebrows, like those of the actress and singer Zendaya. Hers are perfect: they are filled in with the right kind of thickness. I love the slightly enhanced natural look of them. Recently I purchased an

LA Color eyebrow fill-in and stencil kit, but I am afraid to use it. The process will unfortunately require assistance, as I cannot hold the stencil up to my eyebrow and fill it in by myself.

Right now, I think that's all I want to learn with regard to makeup, because the plate feels pretty full. That, and the contouring, foundation, and concealer steps of makeup seem like they will take too long and I am admittedly a very impatient person. Another dream of mine is to get my makeup done professionally. When I express this desire to friends on- and offline, they are surprised it has taken me this long to get it done. I have been told that Sephora does it, but I think the real dream is to have it professionally done and then have somewhere fancy to go like a dinner or a red carpet, but that feels impossible and improbable. Then again, I thought ponytails were impossible and look at me now, proving my own self wrong. I used to believe that makeup could hide my ugly, but now I know that it can enhance what beauty is already there.

The best thing about the ponytails three years later is that they have given me the kind of confidence I never had before, serving as the catalyst to an assurance that everything is going to be okay in due time. Outside of learning how to apply enhancements to my physical beauty, maybe I will drive one day or learn to run again. I like to imagine my feet hitting pavement or grass, heel then toe, heel then toe, the wind on my face and the fear long gone. My best self can get in a car and drive herself to the library to get lost in books, and to the movies to get lost in the worlds of other people on the screen. So much of my life has been spent adapting to my body and then to the world at large. My hope is that the adapting will continue and I will discover new ways to do the impossible, new ways to live a life full of firsts and new loves. My ability to put my hair up didn't change the world, but it changed my world. I saw true possibility for the first time. So much of disability is adaptation and discovering the sorts of tips, tricks, and work-arounds necessary to survive in public and private spaces. In many ways, a work-around ponytail seems superficial, but I urge you to think of the privilege in thinking that way.

Imagine, for a moment, waking up to find that your right arm has 10 percent of its former motor function. Odds are, you'll need to take a second to reassess. You make your way to your bathroom mirror and you wash your face with relative ease due to your fully functioning other hand, but your fingers on your right cramp up as soon as you lift your arm to do anything, really. This is my everyday reality, except I did not wake up one day with 10 percent motor function: this has been my life forever. I don't have the privilege of fully functioning arms and legs, and I say as much not because I think it makes me less than someone who does or because I think it is the be-all, end-all—I don't. I say as much because to live your life not having to adjust the way you enter spaces, the way you do your everyday tasks, because your body is fully functioning at all times, is a privilege. It is not a privilege you can control but a privilege nonetheless. So the next time you are scrolling the internet or watching late-night infomercials and you see something like the Sock Slider or EZ Cracker and think it's ridiculous, I hope you pause and remember the privileges you have, who these things can actually help, and that it is okay to be excited about "trivial" things because life is too short to police anyone else's joy of triumph or innovation. Especially your own joy or triumphs.

The discussion to be had is one about laziness. I was twenty-four when I could properly put my hair up in a ponytail, but I was not lazy for the other twenty-three years I was on this earth. When I wrote about chairs earlier in this collection, I wrote about laziness, the inherently ableist term and the belief that disabled people are inherently so, with and without mobility aids. More important than the culture of laziness is the fear of rest: the idea that we must stay in constant motion in order to consider our days well spent. Now, I love a good motivational saying as much as the next person. The usual suspects: "Hustle hard"; "Work now, play later"; and "Success is 10 percent inspiration and 90 percent perspiration." I get the appeal—sometimes we need these sayings to get motivated to take on the day—but these same sayings operate under the assumption of able-bodied hustling, grinding, and success. We live in a society that often chastises the celebration of tiny triumphs, ones that don't mean working your body to exhaustion or pushing past pain. Some of us can seriously hurt ourselves that way. I would rather be alive with my ponytails than dead from trying to keep up when my body was screaming at me to rest and take it slow, the hustle be damned.

Figuring out how to put my hair into a ponytail did not make me instantly love myself or my body. The learned action was not a cure-all. I would love to be able to tell you as much, but that is not the way that life works, unfortunately. My realization, my epiphany of joy and self-worth, would come at the tail end of 2016, but I understood the importance of that earlier moment. That is the funny thing about breakthroughs: they happen much closer together than we realize sometimes. A domino effect, if you will: hard work can bring triumph, and triumph can bring triumph, or effort can bring joy. I do believe that the past version of myself knew that self-love was possible, and this was going to put me on the right path deep down even if we did not know it yet or want to admit it. After all, change is a very scary thing. Most of it can be very good, like learning to do your own ponytails, finding a new TV show that you love, or making a new friend. The time in-between, though, when you don't know where your feet will land and you are traveling to that change without anything to guide you, is petrifying. The only saving grace is to try our best to remember all the other changes we have made that did wonders for our lives. This, the ability to do my own ponytails for the first time three years ago, and the ability to grow with them now, is one of the good changes worth holding on to in place of the fear.

Now every time I pick up a hair tie I feel that same rush of excitement even after all this time. I don't need to tell you about the magic in achieving something you thought impossible. You know that feeling that starts at your toes and reaches the tips of your fingers? The relief and awe of it all? You are overwhelmed and emotional in the best way, and before you know it, you're smiling so wide your mouth hurts because you feel invincible, indestructible, powerful. Even in this moment, as you think about the thing that gave you this feeling, you can't help but smile with pride. You did the thing you thought you never could, because it mattered to you to be on the other side of your fear; you proved your toughest critic wrong, yourself. That is always worth celebrating, laminating with a picture a moment of silence, a dinner with your friends—big or small, it all matters, and it may feel silly but they are always worth noting. With each ponytail I feel like I am saying yes to growth, to effort, to myself, and it is so exciting to give myself the benefit of the doubt and the chance to say I did and I will make them better. I will master braids and twists, and whatever other hairstyle interests me in the future. I highly recommend saying yes to growth and effort.

I no longer have to ask my sister for help unless I want a ponytail that will last a while or a touch of makeup, because even as a person who is learning, sometimes I just need the job done right so I can be as cute as possible at whatever function we are attending. My hope is that I won't always have to look to Leah to put a lasting foot forward, and I am excited for that possible future in which we are living apart and I can FaceTime her my look for the night to see her beam with pride because she knew when it was a work in progress. When *I* was a work in progress. My ponytails feel like a revolutionary act, a celebration of disability and of me. I will never blend in, and I am recognizing the beauty in that fact. However, with my ponytail and red lip, I feel less like an outsider and more like the badass, black disabled feminist I am.

Search: What's wrong with me? Absolutely nothing.

THE PRETTY ONE

All my life I have wanted to be beautiful. I long to be desired by readers of magazines and audiences of movies and TV shows. My heart has raced as I watched red carpets and closed my eyes to imagine myself there, too, in those designer dresses and jumpsuits, smiling arm in arm with Reese Witherspoon, Oprah, or Mindy Kaling long before they starred in *A Wrinkle in Time* together, because in these fantasies we are friends, genuine ones who can talk about anything. When we first met, they had their questions about my disability as people often do, but we talked about it and moved on. They never wanted brownie points for being in my life. In these fantasies, my body and my face were on Getty Images the next morning, my name on all the best-dressed lists. I still dream of this. I long for the custom dress designed by Christian Siriano, Carolina Herrera, or Zac Posen. My friend Danielle and I text each other during red-carpet award shows just to fawn over the outfits and discuss which ones we would love to wear. Beauty for me is just as much about fashion as it is about anything else. I do not have the budget I need for the fashion I love, for the aesthetic I dream of, but even if I did, you don't see bodies like mine on your red carpets, in your movies, and on your TV screens. You don't—but you will, because I am coming for them.

There are many people who believe that discussions of beauty are futile and unimportant. I am not one of those people. I understand that there is more to a person than his or her physical appearance, and I agree with this, while I also understand that we live in a society and culture that give physical attractiveness real weight and merit. There is nothing wrong with recognizing your own beauty or the beauty in others and, with consent, speaking about that beauty. The intricacies of beauty and the decisions of who is and isn't beautiful fascinate me. As a disabled person, living in a disabled body, I am not supposed to be beautiful, but I have been proving people wrong all my life, so why stop now? The truth is, most people don't expect you to feel beautiful or to think of beauty on any level outside of envy as human beings. History shows that when you ask most people about what they think is beautiful or attractive, you won't find disability on their lists.

Believe it or not, I get it. I once felt that way, too, the deep desperation for distance from my disability. My disability was supposed to be a thing that people could learn to ignore or pretend didn't exist long enough to learn to love me. After all, that's what I was doing, trying my best to ignore it in the hopes that it would get bored and go away, so I wasn't going to blame others if they decided to do the same. I learned later how ridiculous the notion was, and it didn't work. No one learned to love me anyway, or thought I was beautiful enough to ask out on a date to prom. I was never the belle of anyone's ball or the girl who got the guy at the end of the movie. The real happy ending came when I decided I loved myself even if no one else did—and I still do. That is why I celebrate beauty and fashion, because of the evolution I have had with both industries. The envy is still there in some ways, but so is the knowledge that my beauty is just as worthy and valid as conventional beauty. The ideology of waiting for anyone to see past part of who I will be forever was flawed and wasted too much time and energy in the long run. Nevertheless, there is a conversation to be had about beauty and disability, and this is just one of many.

As I said, I love clothes, the way they feel, look, and smell. The way that you can tell the world who you are and what you are all about with the right piece of fabric. Clothes are a reflection of who we are and what we love, but often clothes are not designed with bodies like mine in mind. Most clothes are designed with the symmetrical and able-bodied in mind. There is also the issue of designer clothes being tailored to sizes four and under. They are not designed for disabled or fat bodies, and especially not for anyone who is both fat and disabled. I am a person with a physical disability who does not need a mobility aid, but shopping is even worse for the members of the disability community who do. I can go into a store and find items that I can work with; they'll still have issues in terms of buttons and clasps that are hard to fasten with the full use of one hand and the limited use of the other, and there is the length of time it takes me to get dressed due to my limitations in range of motion, but I make do. Some of my friends, however, require tailors, and so they end up paying for their clothes twice: once at the store and again to have them tailored to fit their bodies. The costs add up, and it is frustrating because we give this industry our money only for our needs to be ignored.

Thankfully, things are starting the slow climb to change. There is Tommy Adaptive, which is a Tommy Hilfiger clothing line made for people with disabilities. When the brand launched in 2017, I was a part of its fashion incubator, providing it with feedback on the line: we focused on the fit, feel, and look of the clothes in exchange for the clothes themselves. What I loved most was that fashion wasn't sacrificed for function in the way it often is with other adaptive clothing lines. There is also Zappos's, Target's own Cat & Jack (a clothing line for kids with disabilities), and companies like Open Style Lab, which is doing great work for people of all abilities. Yet and still, there are issues with each of these companies, as there are with most things. Tommy Adaptive has a higher price point, which is in tandem with the company's other lines and its mission to not otherize Tommy Adaptive from the style and quality of those lines. Zappos at this point has only athleisure wear, and disabled people need more than that. Cat & Jack is for children alone, and those children will one day grow into adults who won't have the option to shop that line anymore, and Open Style Lab is based in New York City, so if you don't live in that area, access is an issue. I do not think the onus is on these brands alone, and I commend them all for even putting forth the effort. My hope is that they will inspire other brands to start catering to my section of their customer base. I have loved clothes forever; now I am waiting for clothing brands and designers to love me back. Clothes were once a tool I used to hide away from the world and to try my best to go unnoticed, but now they are an extension of me and my newfound confidence. They aid in my feeling beautiful, sure, and understood. They are a reflection of my excitement to be alive and relatively well. I no longer need them for armor—they are now my crown, which no one can ever take away from me.

The same love I have for clothes, I have for magazines. This love is a part of why I became a writer. Like most people, I spent my teenage years with posters from magazines on my wall. There was the collage of Usher posters that I ruined a few months later in an attempt to save them from possible retaliation after I ripped one of my sister's basketball posters off her wall in unjust anger, and a Jesse

McCartney poster on my closet door. There were the pictures of my favorite celebrities and their cute clothes that I coveted and held on to to browse through when I was bored. Magazines felt like magic in my hands, because I longed to be important enough to be in one, standing arm in arm with my favorite celebrity best friend while we laughed and pretended as though our photo wasn't being taken. I read the quizzes about the bad boy most suited to be my boyfriend, the embarrassing "it happened to me" stories about girls passing gas or burping in front of their crushes, and articles about the must-have accessories for fall. I wanted to be as beautiful as the celebrities in the pages and on the covers. I wanted to know what conventional attractiveness felt like for at least one moment, to know that I was the envy of someone else.

....

As I grew older and the belief that anything felt possible left my consciousness, I stopped thinking it was possible for me and my body to find itself in magazine pages and on covers and started focusing on the dream to find my name above a glossy article inside them instead. I love being in print even as a writer with a lot of content on the Web. I used to work at a digital fashion and entertainment magazine called *Cliché* magazine, and I loved it. Even though the position was remote and I worked from home, I had a wonderful editor in chief named Megan Portorreal, and I loved writing to PR clients that I was a writer at *Cliché* magazine. I smiled every single time I wrote out the word *magazine*, as if it were transferring its magic to me. The younger version of me was amazed at some of the celebrities I was able to interview in my time there, and while no interview ended in a friendship, I felt like I was living out one of my big dreams. To this day, I still have a soft spot for magazines, especially the mainstream ones like *Cosmo*, *Essence*, *Vogue*, *Teen Vogue*, *Harper's Bazaar*, and *Glamour* (I had the privilege of having an article in its print issue). I still long to see myself and my body on their covers and in their pages, celebrated by a world ready to embrace and respect disabled bodies.

My greatest hope is that that day comes in my lifetime, because our bodies are beautiful and we deserve to shine. I am excited by the changing tides, the effort to include bigger bodies in fashion conversations, and the era of speaking up and pushing back when something is offensive or exclusionary, and I believe social media is a huge factor in this change and ability to be heard by a wider audience—but there is still work to be done. The fact is that beauty is subjective: what is beautiful to one person might not be to another and vice versa. The idea holds merit, but it is also harmful because what does it mean when the only thing that we deem beautiful is thin, white-skinned, and able-bodied? For those of us (so, most of the world) who live outside that ideal, are we to believe we are ugly and unworthy of celebration? I don't think so. I think it is time to shift that ideal and start looking outside our own circles and into others to discover a different type of beauty, a different brand of beauty.

Speaking of beauty brands, you don't often see disabled people in their ads or on their websites. In the off chance that you do, the chosen person—never *persons*—is a wheelchair user. I do believe that my community members who are wheelchair users deserve representation, too, but there is also this preconceived idea that disability stops and starts with the use of wheelchairs. I am living proof that this is not true, yet you don't see people like me in those ads, because as it is now, I do not exist in the eyes of the fashion and beauty media or in the design of companies' products or clothing.

This will change—mark my words—but for now, this is where we are, reckoning with the fact that even when we find the confidence to love ourselves, the world still has some work to do in recognizing our rights, our worth, our beauty, and marketability.

Many in our community, myself included, have made multiple efforts to point this out but the words fall on unwilling ears. We talk a lot about inclusion, but the moment we mention disability, most able-bodied people without an invisible disability or chronic illness think we are taking it too far. That is a direct result of ableism, whether these people realize it or not. To the people with disabilities who feel the same, it may be because of internalized ableism. Fear, ignorance, and misinformation breeds ableism, and ableism breeds abuse: physical, verbal, and emotional. When I asked on Twitter for our inclusion in beauty ads I saw this firsthand. My words were met with such pushback that I considered leaving Twitter for good. I had received pushback before on the platform whenever I mentioned representation in film and TV for disabled people of color, but this was on an entirely different level. The tweet: *Where are the disabled people in your beauty campaigns?* The response: a flurry of tweets that called me everything from a crippled bitch to a Rihanna hater. (I love Rihanna, for the record; she is amazing. I want to make that clear: we love Rihanna in this house forever and always, amen.) The tweet wasn't about her Fenty beauty ad, which featured Rihanna in the beginning before quickly cutting to models with varying skin tones wearing the makeup line to tease all of the shades that would be available. The teaser ad received both verbal and written praise from fans and publications alike, as it should have. The only issue I had was that I hadn't even seen it when I made the tweet. But often, once Twitter users get ahold of something, they don't let it go. My tweet was about a larger issue—the issue of disabled bodies not being seen as beautiful enough to showcase despite the fact that disabled people buy makeup, too. Disabled people are the last to receive any ounce of consideration, and that is the truth, even within the community. If you are not white and disabled, you often receive even less than the scraps that the white disabled community members receive. Sometimes, life in that way feels like a never-ending fight for acceptance or even mere acknowledgement of one's lived experiences. Someone to say, "We see and hear you, and we are going to do something to change it for the better."

While I was being made into memes and told to jump off bridges, these fans were proving my point. They refused to read the rest of the thread, in which I explained the overall problem, because I think confronting privilege is tough for everyone, myself included. There is something hard about admitting privilege when you are seen as the disenfranchised minority in so many other ways. That's what hurt the most about the tweets: that they were being made by other black people who should have understood what a lack of representation does to a person or people—and I do in fact believe these people understood this—but instead they just thought it was a funny thing to joke about or get on me for. When disability is seen through the lens of a joke, those same people making the jokes are less likely to listen to disabled people when we speak or acknowledge the valid point of a culture that is fine with taking our money but would rather we hide away in the shadows. That is the true issue at hand. To critique something or someone you love is to understand that your love for it doesn't mean it cannot be made better or improve on what made it great in the first place. Change is as much about self-introspection as it is about the collective change. In fact, one is not possible without the other.

As a black disabled woman, I know that there is much to improve on in my personal life and in the world at large. There are people in the world who have gone all their lives without seeing themselves represented and without feeling like they have the ability to be and feel beautiful. Often when those people say as much, they are told that they have become too greedy, that they are asking for too much. The people who declare that we are greedy for wanting more and better are completely forgetting what it felt like for them to feel invisible only months and years earlier. In order for true change to occur, we can't just stop at the inclusion of ourselves; we have to try and fight for everyone, because no one should feel like who they are is not enough. Living as and in a black disabled woman's body, I know that I can never be one and not the other, and that's where the double rejection stings. I am often reminded that it is not just my disabled body that people find unsightly, but that the addition of my black skin causes conversations to pause around who should be featured in what campaigns and why. The conversation about beauty and fashion cannot happen without the discussion of race.

....

The funny thing about race is that it affects almost every system and area of the world in one way or another, whether we'd like it to or not. I am black all the time. There are no days off from blackness (and I don't need any). What black people need is respect in every space. There is an exhausting process of entering public spaces never knowing how your blackness will be perceived by the people who are not black—and what the cost of that perception may be. The wave of inclusion of people of color in fashion and in the world of cosmetics is fairly new. Brands in cosmetics and clothing are having to think about the backlash they will receive if their lines don't feature shades or clothes for a wide-ranging customer base. Rihanna's Fenty Beauty really shook the table in that regard when it launched forty shades with the promise to add more, in the face of other makeup brands, which have four or five shades, the majority of which cater to different white skin shades, and two base shades for people of color that end up not even fitting us all. When we stopped accepting the bare minimum and gained an audience behind our voices, things got better, but there is still work left to do. We need to combat and change the preconceived notion that white and whiteness is pure while black or anything else is not. When Tarte released its highly anticipated Shape Tape foundation, its customers of color were disappointed to discover that all they received during the initial launch were two shades in hydrating and matte foundations. Tarte apologized after the criticism went viral, and it promised to finish more shades and release them when they were ready. Dove, a company that isn't makeup but skin care, released a commercial in 2017 in which a black woman was the symbol for the "before," with cracked and brittle skin, and a white woman the "after," with moisturized skin. The brand apologized swiftly and pulled the ad, but if there had been some black people in the room during the advertising discussions, maybe all that could have been avoided. The same thing is true for the Pepsi commercial with Kendall Jenner, in which a model with obvious connections to the fashion industry leaves a photo shoot to end a Black Lives Matter–type protest by opening a can of Pepsi while people of color stand behind her cheering.

If diverse voices outside the white experiences saw these ads before they were approved, maybe they could have been left on the cutting room floor. When you don't have people in the room who have lived through experiences that mirror what you are trying to sell or people who can bring more diverse ideas and experiences to the table to help you see people you may have not seen otherwise, this is the result. Having to ask to be included is exhausting most days. Having to hope that someone will see your humanity and see past their implicit biases takes a lot out of any person. The practice ties back to the way we love the things that do not always love us back. (There is also the worry that brands do these things because they know by now that the controversy will bring traffic to their websites, thus creating revenue. We all hope that the road to these mistakes is paved with good intentions, but sometimes it is easy to infer that it isn't, to remember that at the end of the day these companies need to make a profit, whether through inclusion or controversy.)

Skepticism aside, there have been strides in the right direction. Models like Jillian Mercado have been getting steady work with influential brands. Some of these brands include Olay, Nordstrom, Diesel, and Beyoncé's Ivy Park athleisure line and, with the push for diversity, we are seeing more people of color on magazine covers, and in their pages, and as the faces of or in partnership with cosmetics companies. The progress is great, but colorism is still an issue today. Though we see people of color in these spaces, we often see only those of us who have lighter hues, because people with darker skin aren't given the extra late seat at the table in an effort to try to be more inclusive. That's the thing about using tape to patch a wound: eventually the tape will wear and you start to realize that it isn't enough, that a full reconstruction is necessary. We must rebuild the systems of beauty and fashion in order for true inclusion and equality to occur. I know that I cannot dismantle and reassemble these systems alone; I will need help, and together, change will be possible.

In order to change who and what we see in these industries, we have to talk about why we see the bodies that we do in the first place.

In college, one of the first things I learned in my media and communications class was that when it comes to advertising, sex sells—and it does. Just look at any perfume or cologne ad, and you'll see that it is filled with sexual innuendo. The conversation about advertising and sex as they relate to disability and beauty as well as fashion and race is important, because they are all connected. We already know that fashion and makeup companies do not think of the disabled body, in part because of ableism. The other reasons may be because we live in a society and a media landscape that don't see disabled bodies as sexy. We are only to be pitied, and if we are black with a disability, we are feared—because our blackness comes first, and it is understood through prejudices and learned racist behavior that blackness is scary. The biggest issue is that there isn't just one issue to tackle for change. Disabled people are sexy regardless of what society may believe, but the fact that there is an able-bodied, thin, or "curves in all the right places" bias in advertising is the problem we need to address at the same time. And in the off chance that we see, say, a black woman in advertising, she is usually lighter skinned, famous, conventionally attractive, and hypersexualized. Yes, hypersexualized no matter what we wear, how old we are, or what we are doing.

....

In discussing the ways in which the hypersexualization happens, the reasons and the history are imperative. It starts when we are young. Black girls don't ever really get to be black girls. The moment we start to develop breasts or a butt, the moment puberty decides to show up, we lose all traces of girlhood, all perceived innocence. There is the catcalling by men who are often twice the age of the girl they are catcalling. There is the envy of black women's curves by those who don't have them, and that envy lends its way to racism, as it did for Demetria Obilor, a traffic reporter in Texas who went viral because viewers said she looked "ridiculous" with her curvy body and "unprofessional" hair. Her dresses weren't too short and her hair was done, but many viewers couldn't seem to get past the fact that the dresses hugged her natural curves. Stories like these happen all the time—discomfort with curves on black bodies but celebrations of them on nonblack bodies.

The hypersexualization isn't just about catcalls and curvy bodies; it takes form in the belief that young black girls can never be innocent girls. We are assumed to be guilty and are profiled as such under the guise of coded language. Our language and dialect, clothing, and bodies are under constant surveillance, so that if or when we slip up, the ingrained thought emerges: *We told you they were up to no good.* When a police officer was caught on camera body-slamming fifteen-year-old Dajerria Becton in 2015, then–Fox News host Megyn Kelly boldly proclaimed that Becton was "no angel." The assertion that a fifteen-year-old can somehow deserve to be body-slammed by a cop is a direct result of racism and the black-as-dirty/whiteness-as-pure-or-clean practice. I know that we are to believe the best intentions in people, but Fox, Kelly, and an America emboldened by racism, homophobia, and hatred in the highest office do not have to hide behind an empty apology anymore, because their actions are being championed by the inhabitants of the White House. The coded language with regard to brutality and hatred is the same as that in advertising, even if the coded language in fashion and beauty is not as much verbal as it is visual.

The issue with that is that the bodies are being sold with little regard to the people in them, and when we see the hypersexualiza-tion of women and black people and those of us who fall into both categories, it carries an extra sting, because we spent centuries being reduced to our bodies on the fields of plantations during slavery and now, to justify the brutality against black women and men. The structure of representation in the beauty and fashion industries is problematic, to say the least, but so is everything else we consume and enjoy. So, the fight to be represented in these mediums is one that I have always had. I will never claim to speak for anyone else, but the moment that I felt beautiful after twenty-five years of not feeling beautiful, I wanted the world to know.

There will be people who, as I stated earlier, find this request to be excessive, but the fact of the matter is that I cannot and I will not parcel off sections of my identity in the hopes that one box will be checked. Why not shoot for the stars? It is true that the small wins matter, black cover girls and supermodels matter; it is exciting to watch them shine and grow. I feel the same about black actresses and actors, because I have always believed in the magic of entertainment. As I am a self-professed popular culture fanatic, acting is a secret passion of mine. When other black people win, I feel like I win, but why must I have to look at other bodies in mainstream media, in beauty and fashion, to find a win? When will I be able to look at my own body or a body like mine and smile, because she made it to that commercial, that red carpet, and that makeup contract? I hope that day is soon. I know that I am working tirelessly for representation in all forms of media, with the softest spot and the brightest sliver of hope for the entertainment, fashion, and beauty industries, because they are my favorites.

In knowing why things are the way they are and why change is not only welcome but necessary, we can focus on how to make the change plausible and on the work that is being done already. When I started #DisabledAndCute, I didn't think about the fact that it could become a part of the beauty conversation. In fact, it wasn't until weeks later that I realized it was being brought up in beauty circles. As I have said before, it started as a celebration of self-love and became a movement of its own after it went viral. I am not saying that the hashtag saved lives, but I think that it helped open up dialogues and shed light on biases. I am very proud of that. What I am most proud of, though, is that the hashtag gave disabled people a space and the permission to say *Yes, I feel cute, beautiful*, and so forth, even if it is not currently reflected back in our media. I know that in my life, part of the reason I believed I deserved to feel bad about myself and thought that I was ugly was because I was shown no other way with regard to disability representation. I do not want that for any other young disabled person, those years spent hating mirrors or anything that reflected my face and body. The best society is one that is a true reflection of its inhabitants, and those of us who are not thin, white, and able-bodied are tired of waiting in line. Better yet, one of the first things both beauty and fashion can do is rid themselves of the "ideal" body in the first place.

Keep the traditionally beautiful models and celebrities if you please, but mix the rest of us in there, too. Stop selling the idea that we must adhere to a certain type of beautiful, because that is harmful, a bold-faced lie. If we taught young girls, boys, and gender-nonconforming people that there is nothing wrong with being different and that those differences were beautiful, we could stop using low self-esteem to sell products and start selling those products as enhancements or expressions of what is already there. I truly believe that making people feel good and less like they are trying to mimic an unattainable idea will be much more beneficial morally and financially. I worry for a world that is continuously fed the idea that we must do one billion things for beauty and happiness to be ours. I worry because the models and celebrities we are meant to emulate do not even look like their pictures and ads in real life.

I am not alone in my love for fashion and beauty (though admittedly all that I am good at right now is lipstick, but I am working on eye shadow and brows because my eyebrows are nonexistent and I cannot fully focus on world domination without mastering the three essential basics). The strides that we are making in fashion are great, as small as they may be, but now it is beauty's turn to try and reflect the world we live in and, essentially, the market such companies are actually marketing to. There are other people in my community doing great work with regard to the fight for representation, and we lean on each for support, resources, and the like. Rebecca Cokley (a little person) and Alice Wong (who has a neuromuscular disability) are two professional women who love fashion as much as I do but find that clothes that make them feel and look good are either few and far between or require tailoring. My friend Vilissa Thompson (who has osteogenesis imperfecta, or "brittle-bone disease," as it is commonly known) loves Fenty Beauty foundation, while our friend Maysoon Zayid (who has cerebral palsy) is a "MAC cosmetics girl" because its makeup is easy to use and "every penny of MAC Viva Glam goes to HIV research." So we are all proof that disabled people not only buy makeup and clothes but love them, and we are aware that these things are never just makeup or clothes to us but celebrations of being women, mothers, sisters, friends, and humans. I have always believed that the fashion and beauty industries do not just see themselves as one superficial thing, that they see themselves as multifaceted as human beings are. Whenever I think of these industries, I think about the work it takes to finish fashion lines and the blood, sweat, and tears that go into the science behind makeup formulas. Each designer and creator in these fields has different reasons for loving and being in them; all of them fell in love with something about the industry because they saw themselves or who they wanted to be. This is important, because no one person is the same, and so, year after year, it is surprising and disappointing when the differences and the multifaceted aspects of fashion and beauty are not showcased.

For all my critiquing of the industries I love, I know that the change I desire can't and won't happen overnight. But I want to remain clear that it *must*, and we must strong-arm the change if we have to. The change and the work will not be easy, because most change isn't, but I believe that we will be better for it. When we close ourselves off and celebrate only one type of beauty, no one wins. We miss out on a world of people who are beautiful in different ways. I believe that our beauty and fashion industries should reflect the world we live in and stop expecting us to harm ourselves and our bodies to fit into the ideal created by Eurocentric beauty standards.

On a great day, in the light and under the gaze of a full-length mirror, I know what is beautiful about me and what I have to offer. On the bad days, I can appreciate what I knew to be true on the great days. I am a black woman with beautiful black skin; the fingers on my right hand bend in interesting ways, and they are beautiful, too. Traveling farther down my fingers you will find faded scars on my last three fingers and one large scar in the space between my thumb and finger that took me longer to love. There is a black circle farther down my hand that I hate still, because my love is a work in progress. The entire right side of my body is full of scars from surgeries and falls. They are cool enough to warrant a black-and-white photo series with a clever name, but I am no photographer. A raised scar sits at the base of my hip and travels five to six inches down my right leg, while another small scar graces the inside of my right thigh, perfect for a high slit dress and a red carpet. The left side of my body is not to be outdone by the right. My fingers bend when I wish for them to and the scars on this side come from falls alone, but it is beautiful, too. The sides of my body exist together like yin and yang. The left side does all the real work, but the right side is grateful and helps when it can.

The scars and the working and bent fingers are not the only beautiful things about me. My smile is big and infectious, my lips a little crooked but the kind of full people dream of, my nose an anchor carrying the weight of the glasses that find themselves on its bridge more often than not. I have really nice breasts and shoulders that I like to share with the sun in the summer months, and the kind of belly fat you can grab a handful of. I laugh loudly and sometimes so hard that tears form, which is great for talk shows. It is the kind of laugh that photographs well enough to sell your lipsticks, and all I need is one shot to prove it. My body, in all its imperfections, is what the entertainment, fashion, and beauty worlds have been waiting for; they just do not know it yet. I am funny enough to star in your comedies and humble enough to know that it won't be easy. I have great taste in music, so I will pick the best songs to walk down your runways to and the best images to grace your magazine covers. My loyalty and sense of humor are my favorite nonphysical things about me, as is my love for cheesecake—but that is another essay entirely.

All jokes aside, though I believe all the things I said about myself to be true in the humblest way, I don't want to see change solely for me but also for my people—my people being black, disabled, women, nonbinary, and LGBTQ+. I believe in riding for the people who ride for you, and the people who want to get on board can, but if they don't, you call it a draw and continue on with the work regardless. You see, I am not the only beautiful person in these communities or at these intersections. I am rooting for all of us to have the chance to show the beauty we all possess with regard to both the beauty and fashion industries, but we can't succeed without being met part of the way. The issue is about access, particularly the access we don't have, which is, in part, the result of a combination of racism, sexism, ableism, homophobia, and internal biases. All of this can be confronted and corrected in willing parties.

So much of the harm caused by the fashion and beauty industries results from their incessant need to convince consumers to push for unattainable perfection. The desire to look like these "perfect" people wearing these perfect clothes has led to people doing drastic things to their bodies in an effort to mold them a certain way. This marketing ploy has led to eating disorders in both women and men, the businesses within each industry competing to have the skinniest models, the best celebrity spokespersons, and the most carefully curated social media accounts. They created a culture of dangerous desire, but together, we can fix it. These companies can be more inclusive and mindful in the way that Tommy Adaptive, Zappos, Cat & Jack, and Open Style Lab are, or they can continue to ignore a mostly untapped market, untapped potential, and people like myself, who have always loved both industries but know we could love them more if we saw in them more people who looked like us. Beyoncé said it best in "Haunted": "Perfection is so . . . mmm," and what she means is that the idea of perfection is so boring, so overdone and dated.

Why shouldn't we celebrate imperfections in the discussions of fashion and beauty? They are much more fun and realistic. The imperfections are some of the sexiest and most intriguing things about a person. We already know that imperfect things and people can be and are beautiful and are worth celebrating because they are as messy as life often is—and isn't that what fashion and beauty are all about? The complicated, complex, and stunning whirlwind we call life? All my life I have longed to be beautiful, and I am now. Maybe I always was. Either way, it is time for the fashion and beauty industries to catch up—or get left in the dust.

AN ODE TO THE BOYS

The first man outside my family I ever loved was Stevie Wonder. I was obsessed. I listened to "Superstition" on repeat like it was my job. I doodled "Mrs. Wonder" in my notebooks. I was overly excited when he was on my TV screen. I chose to talk about him for a fourth-grade music project, and I was mortified when the CD I brought in for background music, and a bit of extra effort, skipped as I talked about how cute and talented he was. When I spoke about his May 13, 1950, birth in Michigan, I did so with hearts in my eyes. My mother, to her credit, let me dream of being Stevie Wonder's wife at just seven years old because she knew I had no idea what being a wife meant. I held on to this love for him even after I found out he was married and already had children.

As I grew older, my love for Stevie faded, replaced by love for Brian McKnight. I loved Brian for the same reasons I loved Stevie: he could sing and he had the nicest smile. The true magic of a love song is the ability to make a young girl fall in love with the lyrics of said song when she doesn't yet really understand what is being sung. My standards were a bit low back then. I used to tell myself that he had written his hit single "Back at One" about me, choosing to sing it loudly and proudly whenever I heard it on the radio. When

I was old enough to understand the lyrics of his songs, I laughed at my younger self for feeling so moved by them and at his decision to make music for porn; but hey, someone has to do it, so why not the man who was masterful with the art of the love song in my formative years?

My love for Brian became a love for the R&B superstar Usher Raymond after the release of his second album, *My Way*. The love I had for Usher was deeper than the one I had for both Stevie and Brian because I was older, around eight or nine, and convinced I knew what love was despite being young enough to have heard the word *sex* but without the understanding of how sex happened. My love for Usher lasted well into middle school (where I learned the truth about babies), through high school, and into my junior year of college. I loved Usher longer than my previous crushes not only for his abs and voice but because I thought, from what I saw on TV and his concert DVDs, that our personalities would mesh well. I fell out of that love because I started liking his music less, but I will always remember the time we had before, with all the posters and songs that I was convinced were about me.

In the end, the love I felt for these three men whom I've never known introduced me to the ability to love both real and fictional men with vigor and confidence, even though I knew and know they will never love me back.

There are a lot of people in the world who are real and who will not love me back. I don't necessarily blame them; they have their reasons, but I often miss what I have never really had. Isn't that a strange thing? I am like that line from *The Wedding Date*: "I think I'd miss you even if we never met." First of all, what a beautiful line. Second of all, I get it. Something or someone has such a pull on your life that it feels impossible to imagine your life without them in it. My thing is love: I miss being in it and the security of it without ever having had it. I miss the way it feels, tastes, and is. This missing something I don't truly know may be possible, if only because it feels like I do through the stories of the people in my life. I am used to longing—longing for accessibility, for rights, for access to the spaces where I can advance my career, longing for the end of ableism and harassment online. I longed for one more moment with the loved ones I have lost, longed for the will to live, and for the opportunity to write across genres.

However, this longing is harder to navigate the more time I go without having romantic love to call my own. The longer I am without it, the less hope I have it will come. For a new optimist, I am still pretty pessimistic. The sadness might come from age, watching all my friends go on dates and getting engaged before we're dancing and hugging for Instagram pictures at their weddings. I look to the love in romantic comedies and dramas to navigate what I might expect when someone hopefully decides to love me. James McAvoy in *Atonement*, or James McAvoy again in *Becoming Jane*, makes for the perfect pull of love and loss. Nothing says heartbreak like the scene at the end of *Becoming Jane* when Jane Austen (played by Anne Hathaway) and Tom Lefroy (McAvoy's character) meet again for the first time in years. His lips set themselves in a thin line, but his eyes give him away. They are glossy and apologetic under the weight of what could have been. He has named his daughter after Jane. The surprise and shock are evident on Jane's face; she locks eyes briefly with him. His voice cracks and a strangled "Jane!" leaves his lips as his daughter pesters the author to read from *Pride and Prejudice*. It's this palpable emotion that makes the tears come easy when I watch *Becoming Jane* and that makes it one of my favorite movies.

The stars of these movies stand on their book covers in an array of positions in which my body will never find itself. Their hands are on their hips challengingly; they laugh and gesture. Most are happy, clutching a costar with a wide smile. Others are sad and pensive, their hands clasped neatly in front of them or placed behind their backs. But it would take me a while to get my right hand to cooperate long enough for me to put it behind my back. I cannot pull off the sexy and dangerous pout, either. My black disabled body—with its aching bones and bent fingers, a right leg that is an inch shorter than the left, with its limp and limited motor skills—is not the body reflected on the screen. My body and I have never experienced the scenarios that elicit the emotions on the DVD boxes. I watch these films but don't know what it is like for another person to leave me feeling sexy, dangerous, or happy, or the pain of lost love. I have never been in love. I have never found myself on the receiving end of a lover's arms wrapped around me at the end of a long day; the scars on my right hand and arm do not get kissed after I trace them in apology for the years I spent hating them. There are no weekends in bed with a lover, punctuated with slow kisses and takeout. I have not been promised forever while sweet nothings are whispered into my ear on a Friday night in the passenger seat of an old Camaro. I can only imagine a time in which I held the gaze of a man eager to find his lips on my collarbone. I love my scars, but my love is the only love they know.

My knowledge of romantic love is a love imagined and filtered through an enjoyment of romantic comedies and dramas. Movies are a way to experience lives that are different from our own, a way to see ourselves reflected on a screen, or to see everyone but you reflected on that very same screen. The body I often wish I had belongs to too many black girls to name. Or rather, I wish that my body was considered attractive enough to be coveted the way that their bodies are. This body of mine is not the body that finds itself in pictures alongside the aforementioned beautiful black girl celebrities or above comments that read "You are beautiful." We don't celebrate my body, the *we* of society and the *me* that up until end of 2016 did nothing but despise my body.

In the world of Tumblr, Instagram, and Twitter fame, I find myself desperately wishing to be pretty enough to warrant the praise of strangers, wishing for the option to be someone's #WomenCrush-Wednesday. As artificial as the adoration may be, it is more than I have ever been given. Instead, I find myself dodging white men older than my fifty-three-year-old mother who park themselves in my mentions or direct messages to racialize my apparent beauty and make me wildly uncomfortable. The question is: Where is that same energy from someone my age or closer to it? I feel cute now, even worthy of adoration or a shot at love, but I haven't had one yet. I often ask myself, "Why can't I be beautiful, too? Is there anyone in my age bracket willing to "take one for the team?" Or, "Would it be so bad to fall in love with me?" Now, I don't think so: I feel like a catch most days. I am funny, loyal, and excitable. I love books and music and the smell of gardenias. I have got to be someone's dream somewhere.

....

The first boy (now man) who was my age whom I thought I loved would never return my romantic interests. The reason the word *thought* is necessary is because I didn't really know much about him. He was cute and nice sometimes, and I thought that was enough back then. (I had thought the same thing about Stevie, Brian, and Usher, so old habits die hard.) Let's call him Harry. I knew Harry for a while. We shared classes in intermediate school and hallways in high school. He was kind to me during our middle school years and distant but contradictory in high school. I think he felt sorry for me, but there is no real way of knowing these things. I took his kindness as clues that he liked me, too, with my best friend at the time as my hype woman. I took all the opportunities I had to talk to him. I tried to change myself into a girl I thought he might like. In intermediate school that meant changing the places I shopped. In high school, I wore what I wanted but tried my best to be friendly with his friends in the hopes of being accepted by them and, in turn, by Harry. I took his frequent lingering looks and rare acts of concern or questions about the men in my life as indicators that I was getting closer to being good enough for him. He watched me often, pressed against lockers on the opposite side of the hallway, his friends tapping his arms in jest as I passed by them. He spoke to me in the comfort of empty hallways, always rushed and infrequent. He didn't like seeing me with other boys but he never chose me. The girlfriends he chose were always beautiful, unaffected yet kind, and I couldn't hate them even though I tried. I was never good enough, never pretty enough, never worthy enough of his public affection. He liked the attention more than he ever liked me. I know that now.

As we entered our junior year, I fell out of whatever it was that we were or weren't. I grew tired of the contradictions and vowed to find someone in college to love me in a way that he was never going to. I left those high school hallways behind, confident that someone in college would either love me for who I was or take one for the team until he learned how to love me, even if *I* had not learned to love myself at that point. I haven't thought of Harry in years, until this moment. Wherever he is and whoever he is with, I hope he is happy. I am thankful for his rejection because he was never my destiny. He was just one of the roadblocks along the way.

Despite the pseudoconfidence with which I entered college, I suffered the same fate of undesirability there that I had lived with in high school. Except in college, things were worse. There wasn't even a boy who liked the attention from me. Instead, they mostly just shot me down and left me alone. I went in expecting more—fireworks, dinner dates, nights crammed together in a twin-size dorm-room bed, talking until sunrise. I expected arguments between classes and coffee dates at Starbucks with the false promises of forever. What I got instead was the drunken laughter of boys loudly remarking how funny my limp was and how attracted they were to every girl in our program but me. I had my first real kiss during my senior year of college, right before Christmas break, in a darkly lit bar. The guy who kissed me was drunk and so was I. He was balding and a townie, but again, I was desperate and drunk. I wasn't drunk enough not to be able to consent. However, if I could go back and stop myself from kissing him, I would, because when it was over, he told me that he had done it only as a favor to his friend, who was interested in one of mine. "You seem like a nice enough girl, but I'm not interested" were the last words he spoke to me. I think the constant rejection made my depression worse. I felt like I had no control over my life and turned back to disordered eating—specifically, food restriction. I thought that a thinner body might change people's minds; it did not. All that the restricted eating did was make me sadder, because I missed cheeseburgers and pizza.

We all have things that we know well enough to speak on. For a long time, I believed romantic love was mine. I wrote poems and stories, hoping that if I wrote about it well enough it would come to me and I would no longer have to lie to convince readers that someone wanted me, so that they wouldn't feel sorry for me. Readers were probably tipped off by the fact that the things I wrote, especially the poems, were so bad that any real writer or poet with experience in love would know that love isn't all clichés from movies. Love has evaded me, slipping between my fingers and sneaking through shadows, but I refuse to give up. I like the idea of having to work for it—at least, I do most days. If I have to work for it, the wait will be worth it. Sometimes I worry that love doesn't like me, as though I am still a young girl in middle school desperate to be liked by the popular kids. I know now that people with disabilities can be and are romantically loved, and I have to remember that when I feel myself giving up or getting down on myself. On my worst days with regard to the subject, I revert back to my former self's thinking: *Love is not possible for a girl like you. You are to be tucked away and kept out of sight.* I know that version of myself is wrong even when I start to believe her again. Still, I find myself holding out hope for romantic love, no matter how impossible or naive that hope may be.

There is a part of me desperate enough to try and find love via dating apps. Recently I created three profiles. The first was Coffee Meets Bagel, the next was Bumble, and the last was Plenty of Fish. I never finished the POF profile, deleting it after deciding that three was too many. For Bumble and Coffee Meets Bagel, I wanted to see if my disability was a huge factor in whether or not I was swipe right–worthy . . . and it was. On Coffee Meets Bagel I posted full-body pictures, and the only matches I received were either really old men or disability chasers who said they wanted to "try me out and tell [their] friends." On Bumble, where I posted only selfies, I received matches from people my age. I received four in total in my three weeks on the site, and two of the four who responded to my greetings said they had googled me and weren't interested. One of them was "kind" enough to say, "You were cute in those pictures but the whole cripple thing feels like a lot." When you google me, full-body pictures show up pretty early in the search. After feeling the weight of defeat, I deleted the apps from my phone. Maybe the love of my career and the work will lead me to meet the right person. If I end up back on one of these dating apps, though, don't judge me. I am already doing it enough for the both of us.

....

I have never been in love, but I do know love. My family loves me. I don't have to ask them to; I just know that they do. They pepper me with compliments I am now learning how to take. They also know how to call me out on my bull—and there is a lot of bull. My family is fiercely protective and equally proud. They are unafraid to call out strangers they catch staring at me and wish that I didn't constantly compare my body with theirs. In their eyes I am as pretty as each cousin and sister in our shared squad group message. I am theirs, a product of our late grandmother, Vera Brown, and that makes me special and worthy enough of love in their eyes.

I was self-indulgent enough to ask my mother and sister for specifics on why they love me. My sister loves that I know who I am now, my hair, and that my laugh makes her laugh. My mother loves my ability to work for something until it is completed, my big brown eyes, and that I always seem to surprise her. "There is no end to you," she says to me. I am very lucky to have their love, to know how fulfilling and unwavering it is. I am not self-important enough to keep from you that I was hard to love for years because I felt so sorry for myself and expected my family to as well. I wanted to feast on their guilt; or rather, the guilt I thought they should have.

My friends love me, too, for every day that I hated myself and those in between. In 2014, I went to the San Diego Comic-Con with one of my best friends, Ashley Allcorn. As we walked through the convention center hallways, my body began to ache. We didn't have

time to stop and risk missing the panel we were heading to, and I
didn't have time to stop and cry in the bathroom from embarrassment the way I wanted to. When we reached the end of the line and
sat down cross-legged to wait, I asked her if she was ashamed or embarrassed of me. I did that a lot with my friends before I knew what
it was like to love myself CP and all, constantly panicking about the
day it would all be too much for them to handle before they decided
to let our friendship go. Part of me also used these questions to gauge
how long it might take a lover to see past the disability, too. When
I saw many people in costumes—Avengers, *Orphan Black* clones,
zombies and zombie killers—I was excited but envious. Those costumes they could go home and take off, but this body I could not
exchange for a new one. I was worried that I was sullying the experience of Ashley and our friend Emily, so when Ashley responded that
throughout our seven years of friendship (now, ten) she'd loved me
just the way that I was, I had to fight back actual tears as we raced
to the *Orphan Black* panel. Even though Ashley is not ashamed of
me, I often feel like she and my other friends should be. Ashamed of
me for the way in which my body may keep them from getting free
drinks at bars, may keep unwanted eyes on them, may keep them
from being happy by association. I question why they choose me
when they could have someone else. The questions used to come
because I was sad and miserable, but even in finally liking myself,
I worry about being a detriment to their love lives and happiness
because of my physical appearance.

I fantasize about being able-bodied more than I should. These
fantasies are ableist and they come close to undoing the real work
I do every day to remain feeling genuinely cute. I'd love to spend a
week without having to pretend I don't see strangers so caught up in
watching me limp that they nearly run into things, a week when my

bones don't crack and I don't forget to breathe due to anxiety while walking. I'd wake up to a version of me who doesn't have to plead with her right arm to loosen up long enough to put on a T-shirt. I'd get out of bed and catch a glimpse of a right hand that looks exactly like my left. I'd walk without limping down the hall to my sister's room. We would go on a run, just to see if I could do it. We would race to the end of the block and back, pushing our bodies to their limits. Mine wouldn't give out on me, and the realization would make me cry. After years spent in a body that gave out in college lecture halls, restaurants, and clothing stores, I'd be free of the embarrassment that came with it. This dream body and I could do anything, and we wouldn't just fly: we'd soar. In these fantasies, I forget what I already know to be true: it is possible to soar in a disabled body. I forget in order to imagine a break from a body that is newly cute but still a hot topic for the wrong reasons.

Often my fantasies extend to the idea of a love life, though now I am in my real-life body and fine with it. I could meet the man of my dreams in a coffee shop in Los Angeles, while I order an iced coffee (one cream, two sugars). He laughs at my joke about the moon and the stars walking into a bar even though it isn't that funny. In a different fantasy he is the wingman of a mutual friend who is crushing on the friend I came to their party with. He is there to fulfill his wingman duty and keep me occupied. Instead, we talk all night, long after our mutual friend has blown his shot with the guest I brought to the party. He'll kiss me when the sun rises after every other guest has gone home, and he won't regret it. In fact, we'll find ourselves laughing at how long it took us to do it and make plans for a coffee date later that week. In many ways, these fantasies are a way to rewrite my history. A history where I won't enter a relationship at my age so inexperienced.

I find myself in other fantasies with new men, too. At a wedding in Boston, our eyes meet and he lets three songs come and go before walking over to say hello. He isn't great at dancing but he's better with words, leaving only to grab a slice of cheesecake for us to share. During an elevator ride in Maine we make small talk in a building with too many floors. He lingers when the doors open on his floor. He pauses and smiles: "I'll take the stairs back down." We meet after he steps off the stage at a reading in New York City; his work is beautiful and I wish to tell him as much, but I am too afraid to shoot my shot. I imagine instead the way we would end, hurling words we don't mean at each other just to see the who can hurt whom the most. In my fantasies, I don't have to worry about the placement of my hands or the way I look when I walk away. In place of that worry, I am loved by a man who kisses my fingers and doesn't mind lying in bed with me when my limbs are aching, with a warm blanket and the romantic comedies I love so much. When the reality hits and I realize I have spent too much time in my fantasies, I mourn for the loss of them, for the version of me who gets to call them her home. I mourn because I catch myself getting emotional about conversations and actions that never actually took place—and the thing about fantasies is that they are sometimes very unrealistic, but our range of emotions even for the imagined is not. What does it mean that in order to keep myself from despair, I sometimes live inside my head, inside a world where I am desired by men my age and by people who see my body as worthy of love and desire, people who see me as much of the same?

I am weary of the way in which I long for someone to fall in love with me. As a feminist, I believe in independence and operate under the understanding that romantic love shouldn't be the be-all, end-all of any one person's life. I know logically that I would survive without romantic love, but I hate that I should have to plan to. There is also the fear of never having it, of always being the friend, the one who was never "lucky" enough to find a person to love her, which keeps me awake at night. I think it would be nice to have someone to come home to at the end of a long and stressful day, someone to hold me when the world feels too vast and I need to pretend it is just the two of us for a while. I have always told my friends never to put everything into one person, because if it implodes and you have nothing and no one left, how will you rebuild? I believe that still. Yet I know this is an easier thing to say when you have spent your life on the sidelines of other people's romantic love, friends who go ghost the minute they have a significant other. I am certain that it is hard not to become consumed by one person, especially in the beginning. The whole idea of giving so much of yourself to another person is petrifying, but it would be nice to live life with someone in your corner who loves you in a way that's deeper than friendship but understands and respects how much your friendships mean to you. A person who is comfortable with your family, both blood and chosen, while giving you the room to just be in these spaces. I don't want to love someone so much that I lose who I am and the people I have outside that relationship. The thing that scares me the most is doing that: giving my all to someone in place of the people who were here for me all along. So, the dream is to have and to nurture both.

I cast myself in lead roles. I am the presumably heartless boss who is about to be deported to Canada, like Sandra Bullock in *The Proposal*. I am Drew Barrymore's Josie Geller in *Never Been Kissed*, a talented copy editor turned reporter looking to her past to right her future and advance her career but finding love along the way while she is at it. I am the skeptical and loyal friend who spends a night in New York City with a stranger and his band, searching for my drunk best friend, like Kat Dennings in *Nick and Norah's Infinite Playlist*. I am Mae Whitman in *The Duff* searching for ways to change myself until I realize that who I was all along was enough. I am desired, complicated, and seen as the ideal woman for someone.

I am not afraid of heartbreak. The heartbreak is often my favorite part of these movies. I would not complain if I found myself standing alone in the rain. I am willing to stand in the rain confused and angry, like Elizabeth after Mr. Darcy confesses to loving her for the first time in the 2005 adaptation of *Pride and Prejudice*. I would not be bitter if at the end of my life I found myself separated from my true love, like Keira Knightley in *Atonement*. I could not be upset with such endings when the true joy is in the fact that I had them at all. In all of my years of falling for people who have never liked me back, the heartbreak in discovering that truth is easier to swallow because I never expected them to, not really. Not when I hated me, too, but things are different now.

I was always told that when I learned to love myself, the right person would come along when I least expected it. Maybe he will, but for now I am a little let down by the results. I didn't go into this journey because I thought it was going to solve all my problems. I did it because I was tired of living how I was. It's a strange dichotomy, to love yourself while knowing that no one else does yet. Before I loved myself, I thought I knew why no one loved me, because of my physical disability. After love, I am all out of answers, because the things that I used to hate about myself I like now. I like that my journey has not been easy, because then I would not have my stories to tell. Getting to that place of thought was hard, but so much of my life makes sense in these terms. I do not believe that one must suffer to make art, but in order to move on from my pain, even the self-inflicted pain, I choose to believe that the roadblocks were part of the plan, a necessary evil or a chaotic good. The silliest part of my journey has been that I believed the moment my view of myself changed, the world's view of me would change alongside it. The work isn't that easy and it never will be, so I must wait. I hope I don't have to wait too much longer—impatience runs in my family.

....

While I wait and grow in other aspects of my life, I have to reckon with the truth of having never been in love or loved. On the worst days, I let the sadness of that fact set itself in the deepest parts of me, festering and waiting for a day when I am already vulnerable to show itself. My friends always tell me love is not all it is cracked up to be. They want me to feel better, but they can say as much because they have never been in my situation. They have had love and lost it and loved again. Some of them were able to know that they were lovely as young as middle school. Long after they went through the rituals of young love, the first and last loves, I was still dreaming of my own love story, still hoping for a stellar beginning and an exciting middle but a nonexistent end. The fear of dying alone and never experiencing love is an exhausting thing. Even as I find myself on this new journey of self-love. Even as I find myself trading insults for compliments and trying my best to give other disabled women someone to understand and relate to. I am one woman who is on her way to lasting happiness. A woman who will one day see a world where representation isn't so scarce for women of color like herself in mainstream media. Still, I am one person with a disability that takes some getting used to, and whether I like it or not, we are a society built on the first impression. So far, I haven't made a lasting one, and I don't know if I ever will. I give too much to the act of being desired and loved because I never thought it was possible in this body. I hope that someone somewhere proves the old version of me wrong.

There is also the fear that I am disappointing my community of people with disabilities by admitting that I don't know how to dismiss the internalized ableism of believing that an able-bodied body is better than my disabled body, if only because it is desirable to a wider range of people and doesn't tire as quickly as mine. Why are more people not open to the possibility of dating someone with a physical disability? I ask but I do not know the answer—no one has ever given me a straight one. If I had to take a guess, I would say people are easily embarrassed and they buy into the idea that to proudly date someone with a disability will lead to deserved ridicule. The word *deserved* is key here, because if people did not think the ridicule was deserved despite their belief that they are open-minded, they wouldn't be so decidedly closed off to the idea. Are you open to dating someone with a disability? What do your dating preferences say about you? I am not the only one with a lot left to unlearn.

I can dream as much as I'd like, but there is no guarantee that someone will love me, and that is not only scary but disheartening, because if these words and my fantasies are just that, I'll have to learn to live with it, and I will, but it is going to be so lonely. Still, I want for us all to feel good about ourselves and to know our worth as a community and individuals regardless of who may or may not feel as we do. I champion the people with disabilities whom I have met online. I urge them to speak out, speak up, and love themselves. I am a hypocrite in that some days, I forget how to love myself as a single being, and I am consumed by the wish that someone else may love me, too. In these moments, my sole thought is to work toward being enough to be desired and loved. When I spend too many hours on Instagram liking the pictures of my friends and their partners, or on Twitter watching relationships blossom, I forget that I created a hashtag about finally feeling cute in favor of self-doubt and debilitating worry and sadness. I struggle with admitting that I want to be Mae Whitman in *The Duff*, Cameron Diaz in *Charlie's Angels*, or Mandy Moore in *A Walk to Remember*—or that I relate to Jane Austen (well, the very fictionalized version of her life) in *Becoming Jane*, who lived her life without a marriage or a lover, because I am convinced I will share the same fate.

A thing to know about me is that as much as I love the idea of happy, lasting love, I would also like to experience romantic love so that I can have an understanding behind the vigor with which I belt out breakup songs. We don't even necessarily have to break up for the vigor to come; we can argue and I'll pretend like we broke up until the end of the song. I think anyone ready to love me should be able to handle that. Breakup songs are in a league of their own, the ones about the no-good men who use women for money or fame and the ones whose choices are so bad that there are too many to name them all within the song's lines. Specifically, "He Wasn't Man Enough" by Toni Braxton and "It's Not Right but It's Okay" and "Heartbreak Hotel" by Whitney Houston share these sentiments quite expertly. Three of the classics and the queens of gathering the men who have wronged them together via song and telling them about themselves. For a girl who has never known romantic love, I sure do love a breakup song. The emotion behind it is almost unmatched: the ability to tell a person who wronged you in some way that you are better off without them and thriving despite your initial heartbreak. The best revenge will be your happiness without them, as told by my favorite songs. I can't wait.

I don't know how not to care about the way I am seen. I feed into the standard set by a culture that never intended for me to see myself as worthy, that ignores bodies like mine as though we are blemishes to be covered up or flaws to be fixed. We are neither: our bodies are beautiful. A culture that uses skin like mine often as a token or a tool to keep valid criticism at bay long enough to say, "Hey, we added one. That's something." In truth, stereotypes and caricatures of brown and black people, especially in romantic comedies, are far too common. The "sassy" black best friend, the "spicy" Latina, the "quiet" Asian, all employed to move along the arc and story line of a white able-bodied woman. The something that we get is not enough, and it never has been. At twenty-seven, I am still learning so much about myself, and I don't have everything figured out, but I know that I deserve more representation in the genre that I love than what we do have, which is disabled characters who are plot devices to make the love interest seem like a caring and good person or disabled characters who fall in love and are loved despite (eye roll) disability and then killed off for no justifiable reason but to tug at heartstrings and further an able-bodied character's development.

These days, romantic comedies are making small steps toward inclusivity and feminism. They are poking fun at the idea that a woman is nothing without a man, giving their characters depth and purpose outside of their impending romantic relationships and allowing their female leads to live in worlds where they are in positions of power with autonomy in their lives and workplaces. These are characters who aren't looking for love, even though it finds them. Still, I know that, as a genre, romantic comedies are stunted by racism and ableism. In most cases, when a black girl finds herself in a romantic comedy, she is almost never the lead; instead she is the sassy best friend wheeled in and out of scenes to shout, "Hey, girl!" or some form of "ghetto fabulous" line to encourage her white lead to go after the male lead. She is almost never given a story line that isn't based on the mammy archetype. She is almost never given a chance to fall in love, too.

How are we, black girls with disabilities, supposed to see ourselves as worthy of romantic love, worthy of the chance to feel at home in our bodies and personalities, if the only representation we receive is that of a plot device or a joke? We have no choice but to see ourselves in the able-bodied, often white women who acquire lead roles. We have to find ourselves in their quirky or shy demeanors, their witty and quick humor, their hopes and dreams. We follow them on their journey to find themselves as they unlock an inner strength they've had all along. We see as much of ourselves as possible in these women—and still, it is never quite enough.

The ableism in movies is so normalized that it isn't often brought up in conversations about the things Hollywood needs to change. I have never seen a person with a disability as the lead or supporting character in a romantic comedy. In *Forrest Gump*, Tom Hanks's Forrest literally runs until his leg braces falls off; he comes out on the other side with "perfect" legs, as if redemption occurs only from shedding his disability.

There is one thing that I do know, and that is that I want to be romantically loved. I want to know what it's like to fall in love and trip up along the way like they do in *Love Jones*, *Brown Sugar*, and *The Best Man*. I want to be kissed by someone who likes the way the light reflects off my skin or the way my breath hitches when he says my name. I want to be in love to prove that I am worthy of being loved, all of me, not just the parts of me that society can forgive, not just the parts of me that I can forgive. I want a love that will rival the movies, a love that is raw, imperfect, and real. A love that is mine.

Sometimes I don't know how to reconcile my love of my blackness with my love of romantic comedies. I cast myself in these roles, but I do not wish to shed my black skin in the process. I wish to shine a light on it and watch it glow. I know there is beauty in the things that make us different. There are so many stories left to be told. The good news is that black and brown people fall in love every single day, so there really is endless material. The even better news? Black and brown disabled people fall in love every day, too. We are more than just the friends of the male lead who are used to show a sensitive and caring side of the character who "took care of us when we were abandoned" or loved us "despite" our disabilities.

We often love the things that hurt us the most, and my love for romantic comedies is no different. Despite their erasure of my blackness and my disability, I cannot give up on the genre of film that supplied me with a chance to wish for a love I don't yet know if I deserve. I almost feel it is my duty to love these movies, not just for me, but for the young disabled black girl who might read these words, who is growing up yearning in the same way that I did to see all of herself on-screen. We live in a world in which movies and television are conversation pieces. They shed light on the issues facing our culture. If movies and television can bring about necessary change and allow us to have tough conversations, maybe a young black disabled girl who loves romantic comedies can and will create a movie, and a world, in which she is the lead. Maybe she will be afforded the opportunity for romantic love. Maybe my own love for romantic comedies will someday yield the same result.

Love means a lot of things to me. There is the love of my family and friends, the love of romantic comedies, cheesecake, pizza, music, and the written word. I feel loved in return by these things and people. I love them back, but I long for more. I long to understand and experience love outside that of the familial, the platonic, and the love of good things as gifts to my taste buds and ears. All my life I have watched other people fall in love: at school dances, at bars, in classes, in movies, and in unlikely places. I have witnessed two people click with each other and find their own forever. There are people in my life whose love story is like those in the movies, perfect for the silver screen. In fact, a lot of my most frequent and reoccurring fantasies have in some way happened to someone I know—the weddings and the readings, the parties and the bars. All of them were possible for my friends, except the dancing scenes in movies like *Pride and Prejudice* and *Becoming Jane*. I do not have the time to learn those dances in the hopes that someone might throw a party befitting them and I will meet someone willing to dance with me all night. Sometimes I think back on Stevie, Brian, Usher, and all the boys who would never love me with fondness. When I loved them—or rather, when I thought love was possible without reciprocation—I did not love myself. If they had loved me, maybe I would have never learned to change so that I could then learn to love the person I am living with every day. To be romantically loved feels like an adventure I've been waiting for, for most of my life. To be romantically loved is to experience the creation of magic in real time, and even if it doesn't last, to be in that moment, to sit in that magic, would be enough for me. In truth, I love who I will be more than I like who I am, who I am becoming. If I can continue to love the me in this body and shine my light brightly enough to pull me through even the darkest days, maybe someone outside of myself will follow suit.

THE HUMAN IPOD

....

The first time I heard a song that moved me, I was likely in the back seat of my mom's old blue station wagon with my sister and brother. In all honesty, it was probably a Toni Braxton song. We were all quite fond of my mother's "Un-Break My Heart" cassette tape. I'd like to think that I was bouncing along to it with a slight understanding of the way music would later be such an influential part of how I would save myself. The summer months were always my favorite; we'd pack ourselves into that wagon in jean shorts and T-shirts, just trying to keep cool and seeing who could hold a note as long as my mom could. I was always the first to lose, after singing lyrics I was too young to understand. In those same summers, there were weekends spent at my grandmother's house with a stereo and the tastes of songs on the tips of our tongues. We believed that we would have those moments forever.

I know that I am not the first person in the world to say, "I love music; it saved me." But that doesn't make it any less true. Oftentimes, our most personal stories of loss, growth, and the in-between—the things that make us who we are—are universal. I think that's what makes them so necessary and meaningful. I grew up in a very musical household, but not in the traditional sense. We were not a family of musicians with instruments lying all around the house, but my family sang all the time growing up. We sang in cars, while cleaning, and while cooking. We sang Christmas songs in July and about rainy days under the blazing sun. At my grandmother's house, everything sounded like a song, including the saying of grace before Sunday dinners. I was a child who loved hearing her grandmother sing anything, whether that anything was "This Christmas," "You Are My Sunshine," or mumbling along to the songs on the radio. I knew from a very young age that music would be a very integral part of my life even if I couldn't sing—and I couldn't, but I did it anyway.

Music was and is one of the many ways I connect with my family and friends. When my siblings and I were kids, my mother introduced us to a wide-ranging selection of music. We listened to nursery rhymes and kids' music, of course, but we also listened to Stevie Wonder, Toni Braxton, Janet and Michael Jackson, and Celine Dion. She even threw in a bit of Dixie Chicks, Jewel, and the music she was raised on, which included everyone from Teena Marie to Gladys Knight and the Pips. Just to keep us on our toes.

When I think of my childhood, I hear the chords of songs, the warm tones of voices that are with me today and those that are not. There was music required in chorus and music classes in which I sang, boldly and badly. There were pages of sheet music, from which I would read on risers with other students. Whether I knew it then or not, music was the catalyst to many of the relationships I built as a child. My friends and I used to sit in circles and decide which girl group members we would be. In one such discussion, the group 3LW was brought up. I was black, so I was Naturi Naughton, but I was fine with that because she loved Usher as much as I did. As I've noted before, my love for him was strong. I had every album, his *In the Mix* movie, and the *Confessions* concert DVD. I spent my childhood idolizing these musicians because they seemed so sure of themselves, so clear on what their purpose was. I longed for that same clarity even as a child, so I searched for it in their music.

At the start of elementary school, I began to form my own musical favorites outside the natural musicality of my grandmother's voice and the songs we had been raised hearing. The songs that were of my own choosing consisted mostly of the "happy" songs on the radio, or rather, the upbeat songs I could dance to in the comfort of family only. Then, one day, on a fourth-grade field trip, my aide who helped me with classes but also taught me about life, Ms. Dellaccio (the second of two aides I had in my life, Mrs. Carlson being the first), introduced me to the magic of the legendary Shania Twain, and I added her music to my internal list of music worth loving. I kept this list in my head because I thought that writing it down would make it lose all of its magic, but the funny thing about time is that so much of it has passed and Shania Twain is the only name I remember. As a young girl, I was constantly trying to hold on to things that were supposed to be just mine, but music held on to me, and I liked that I was worth keeping in that way.

I spent my childhood listening to those "happy" artists and a few others like them in a period I call "BD"—"before depression"—when I hadn't yet turned into the jaded teenager that life was sure to make me. During the time of BD, I spent weekends in my grandmother's house taking naps and sneaking sips of her coffee, standing in line with my cousins to lick the spoon of whatever delicious food or dessert she had made, and listening to her tell stories of the times she and her siblings had heard their mother sing. On the days when a sports team she loved wasn't doing well and there was nothing good on TV, my grandmother would sing "You Are My Sunshine" or "This Little Light of Mine," or hum a song she had known as a child. I would give anything to hear her sing again. The closest I've come to doing so is when I play the songs she used to sing. I do not remember her voice exactly, but I remember the way I felt hearing it, and in many ways, it helps me keep her close.

When the era of "DD"—"during depression"—began, I was freshly in middle school and looking for music to both soothe and showcase my angsty young-girl sadness. I gravitated toward bands like Good Charlotte, Simple Plan, and All-American Rejects, like many of my slightly emo and white classmates who were sad without the ability to explain why. This wasn't intentional. I listened to a wide range of music growing up, even in my DD era, but I found that whenever I needed to sit in my sadness and express my angst, I was able to do so with the music of white musicians. I felt right at home in their lyrics and melodies, but I refused to sacrifice my fashion choices to align with their clothing choices. The music carried me through middle school and the days when I did not want to get out of bed or exist in a school full of people I was convinced did not understand me or what I was going through.

That is the funny thing about being young and sad: there is this unchecked confidence and belief that what you are going through, the sadness you are experiencing, is yours alone and no one else knows what it is like to be as sad as you are. The sadness leaves you angry, because you tear yourself apart trying to figure out why you deserve to feel so sad in the first place. If you believe you can't manage the sadness, you'll seek songs that reflect it back to you because they are what you know well, even when the reflection of the sadness feels unbearable. As an adult, spending most days on the other side of sadness, I know now how true that wasn't. Depression is not a punishment handed out to people who did something wrong. Depression is a chemical imbalance that can happen to anyone at any point for any reason, and it is nothing to be ashamed of. There were so many people in my same boat, searching for music that would heal them, too. All I needed to do was reach out, but if we knew when we were young what we know when are older, there would be no stories to tell.

....

Two and a half years later, high school began, and my sadness expanded into a belief of certain undesirability. I was so sure that my body made me into a freak, one that everyone was disgusted by, but through an act of fate I discovered the music of Paramore. I joined the Paramore family during their *All We Know Is Falling* era. The album came out in 2005 and changed my life. In that era, the band members were Hayley Williams, Josh and Zac Farro, and Jeremy Davis. The ten-track album featured songs like "Brighter" and "Pressure" and stayed in my Top 25 Most Played iTunes playlist for almost two years. While the album didn't see a lot of mainstream success, I was sold. I had a song for every occasion. There was "Brighter" for the days when I woke up with hope, "Pressure" for when the mountain of homework became too much, and "Franklin" for when I felt desperate to be anywhere else. Paramore felt and feels like a gift to me specifically, despite their large fan base. My love was solidified with their 2007 follow-up, *Riot!* Taylor York would join the band as the new guitarist, though he'd provided backing vocals on *All We Know Is Falling*. In the year 2007, I was in my sophomore year of high school and the eleven-track album was in heavy rotation. I developed a crush on a boy who would never like me back but played "Crushcrushcrush" on repeat and convinced myself he might. There is not a song on this album that is worth skipping; it is that good, even though it didn't have the powers of a love potion to make that boy like me back within its lyric jacket.

By the time that their album *Brand New Eyes* rolled around in September 2009, I was in my freshman year of college. The year would prove to be one of the hardest of my life so far. *Brand New Eyes* was released on September 29, 2009, and my grandmother would pass away the following month. I leaned heavily on music to get me out of bed and to my classes. I leaned on music to lull me and my tears to sleep each night. The song "Misguided Ghosts" really spoke to my feeling of aimlessness through grief, with lines that talk about trying to figure out where you belong while knowing that it isn't where you feel safest or what is most familiar to you. Grief was a new experience for me at the time, and I had no idea how to navigate it or who I might be when it was over. I felt like a true misguided ghost, as the song's title suggests, trying to find myself again. Paramore's way with lyrics is nearly unmatched. In their music, with each song there is always at least one line that hits you the way good poetry should. They create lyrics that make it okay not to be okay, to feel what you need to feel.

When my grandma passed I turned to the band for comfort and answers. Figuratively, I sewed the hurt they discussed on their songs in my clothes because it weighed the same as my own and I wore it like it was all mine, like only they understood me. I let their songs lead me through guilt, anger, and so much grief. We never learned how to live without my grandmother, but we figured out how to get through full days without crying after a while. I write *we* because they were in this with me fully, even if they did not know it. As a person skeptical of change, I did not need anything else to change in my life if I was going to continue on living without my grandmother. So I was devastated to learn that in 2010, Zac and Josh Farro decided to leave the band. Change is still very hard for me, but when the brothers left the band it felt like another death of sorts. One thing that I am very good at is worrying, so I worried that this meant the end of my favorite band and the end of the music that had made me feel even when I tried so hard to stop feeling anything but my own heartbreak. But then Hayley assured fans that Paramore was making new music in 2011.

The self-titled album era began on April 9, 2013, with the remaining members: Hayley Williams, Taylor York, and Jeremy Davis. I would graduate from college a month later with new music to carry me into the next phase of my life. This time, the song that really moved me was called "Hate to See Your Heart Break," particularly the lines "For all the things that you're alive to feel / Just let the pain remind you hearts can heal." I was moved because the song and album came at a time when I needed to be reminded that there was a light at the end of the tunnel. The song wasn't the catalyst for my self-love, but it made me see that such a thing might be possible. The lines have meant so much to me that I toyed with the idea of getting them tattooed for a full year before remembering my low tolerance for pain.

This next phase of my life included as many downs as it did ups, and the same could be said for Paramore. After graduation, I spent a year and some months without a job or any newsroom or publication willing to take a chance on a black disabled girl fresh out of college and looking for a remote or local position. In 2015, Jeremy Davis would announce his departure from the band, and Hayley Williams and Taylor York vowed to continue with the band, but not before they toured with Fall Out Boy on the Monumentour in 2014. I spent the entire last half of their set crying because I was so excited to finally see them in concert. In 2016, Hayley started off a banner year for me with the announcement that the band was working on its fifth studio album, and by February the news was out that Zac Farro had rejoined the band.

To this day, Paramore is still my favorite band. They are my favorite for their beautiful lyrics and masterful production but more so for the way they make me feel strong and vulnerable at the same time, and for the way they've helped me realize that there is nothing wrong with being both. I have loved them in every era and I will love them forever, for being an anchor in my lowest points and a sort of supportive old friend at my highest. The great thing about growing with a band is going back to their older music when you yourself have grown so much and in many ways, as they have grown, too, with age, time, and wisdom. Paramore's music was my safe haven, an escape from loss, grief, and misery, and when I need it for that again, I will return to those same songs. However, the band and myself are not the same people we were in those early eras, and I can appreciate the songs for what they meant to the younger, sadder, jaded me and appreciate the music from *After Laughter* (released on May 12, 2017) that we have now. The best thing about *After Laughter* is that even with its upbeat eighties vibe, the lyrics are sad as hell. That is a really hard thing to accomplish well, but they did it. The acknowledgment of pain, whether or not it is self-inflicted, is important, and the fact that they were able to share their pain and grief in various forms in new and interesting ways with the world took guts and a lot of self-reflection and growth. I cannot wait to see what happens next for them and the ways in which they will continue to enrich my life with their art.

....

Paramore are not the only artists who have meant so much to my life and journey so far. I became a fan of Demi Lovato after conversations with my best friend, Ashley. She has great taste in music and gave me a CD of Demi's first album, *Don't Forget*. I fell in love with her music immediately, everything from the lyrics to the production. I love these things about her music as much as I love Paramore's. She and I are close enough in age to where I felt like she understood the sometimes-exhausting nature of adolescence—or rather, young adulthood—and the feelings of constant discomfort and uncertainty. Outside of my imagined love fantasies, there is a song on the *Don't Forget* album titled "Two Worlds Collide" that I very quickly dubbed the official song of the best friendship between Ashley and myself. Demi followed up *Don't Forget* with the underrated masterpiece that was *Here We Go Again* in 2009. With this album, I allowed myself to dream of potential love in college. In songs like "Catch Me" and "Stop the World," I imagined me and my future love meeting in a lecture hall, where we would joke about the professor's monotone voice briefly before reconvening at the end of the class to formally introduce ourselves. (Yes, even in my fantasies I did not want to be distracted enough to fail a class.) When me and my imagined love would fight, I'd play "Every Time You Lie" and "Solo" until we would make up and I'd switch to "Remember December." My imagined love and I would go through every aspect of the relationship, or what I believed of one from my knowledge of television, with that album as the soundtrack of our love story. When August rolled around, I was excited to start college in the hopes that I would make new friends, learn, and fall in love, all while listening to the album that gave me hope to keep going.

Over the course of my college career, the romantic love never came, but platonic love in friendships, valuable lessons, and new friends came in its place. Even with these things and people, I was still very sad and felt unlovable because no one loved me romantically, and I was still convinced that it had everything to do with disability. In the thick of my personal depression outside the grief and loss of my grandmother, Demi returned with *Unbroken* in 2011, after a personal battle of her own with depression, eating disorders, drugs, and living with bipolar disorder. At the time, the song that meant the most to me on the album was titled "Skyscraper." The song really did a number on me, because I was feeling beaten up and broken down like the song described, but it encouraged me to keep pushing. Before the song's release, I began a long battle with suicidal ideation and the belief that death was what I deserved, and that song kept me from going through with it. Demi would release *Demi* in 2013 a few days after I graduated from college, and the thirteen-track album was full of songs that were fun and catchy, perfect for the summer months and my desire to keep the excitement and pride of graduating with me as long as possible.

She would follow up *Demi* with *Confident* in 2015, but her 2017 album *Tell Me You Love Me* is where she seems most comfortable, sexy, and sure of herself, both vocally and in terms of her artistic vision. When she released her YouTube documentary *Simply Complicated* on October, 17, 2017, fans were able to see an inside look at the making of *Tell Me You Love Me* and her life today. We also learned that during her *Unbroken* era she was still using drugs, and as a person who had been moved by "Skyscraper," I felt oddly relieved, because I had fallen back into my own disordered eating and depressive episodes after that album's release. Her decision to admit her truth allowed me to feel okay with admitting that recovery is a daily process and relapses are bound to happen, but acknowledging that and putting in work to get better was okay. Even while being in recovery after an overdose in 2018, Demi is better than she has ever been and surer of herself as an artist. We have that in common. I feel like, in many ways, we've grown together, dealt with some of the same issues, and found our way to the other side while understanding the work left to do. Life won't be roses for either of us forever, but if we got through each relapse and tough time once, we can do it again and again.

A small but important thing to note is that both *Tell Me You Love Me* and *After Laughter* were criminally underrated and snubbed by the Grammys the year of their releases. Personally, this oversight feels like a gender bias within their respective genres, as women who are lead singers of bands in genres dominated by men, no matter how quality their work is, are still not taken seriously. Still, Demi Lovato and Paramore have shown themselves to be artists who understand themselves more now than they ever have, and the quality of their music proves that.

....

I used to say that Demi Lovato and Paramore saved my life, but I know now that the statement is not true. Their music was affirming and, in my biased opinion, perfect for my ears both then and now, but I know that the real magic of what they did was allow me to see that I was worth saving and cheer me on while I saved myself. That's the magic of the right music and the right people in the right places. In having to figure out who I was now that I was WAH ("working at happiness"), I turned to music again. I listened to all types of music, from pop punk and rock to alternative, R&B, rap, pop, and more, and I found songs that made me feel like the best version of myself while showcasing the growth I made. Even in my newfound happiness, I will always be a person who loves a sad song. Even as the version of myself who is actively choosing happiness, I find that sad songs are a part of that joy, in embracing the days when happiness will elude me or a good cry is necessary. Sad songs are beautiful in that they represent vulnerability in both the artist and the listener.

We don't have enough of that in the world, and we should. As a black woman, I know that my vulnerability is my strength and my choice.

The practice of choice is very important to me. We make choices every single day about every single thing. I made the choice to be sad and the choice to be happy. I made the choice to fall in love with music, and I made the choice to love a white artist and a white group as a black woman. I know that I am not the sole black fan of each artist, because black people are not a monolith who only like certain genres of music. I in no way believe that this is a revelation; nor did my choices ever really alienate me from other black people. All they did was solidify that I was never in control of the music at parties, which is fair, because knowing me, I would've killed the entire vibe with the saddest songs just because I was really feeling a particular one. These words aren't said with any sort of need to defend my choice. The fact of the matter is that we cannot help what music or what things help heal us. Instead, we should just aim for appreciativeness when we discover what does and what will heal us.

There was a moment when I tried my best to like music that I believed to be "blacker," and that choice was a silly and futile one. I did so not out of pressure from anyone else but out of fear that my choices in music meant something deeper than what it was: just a place to belong, with people who understood my sadness. In loving Shania Twain, Aly & AJ, Justin Nozuka, Jack's Mannequin, Cartel, Yellowcard, and the other white artists on the pop and slow jam radio stations, I did not stop loving Toni, Michael and Janet, Beyoncé, Destiny's Child, or various other black artists. My only fear was that my love for the white artists made it seem as though I was ashamed or scared of my blackness. The fear in many ways was because I had done other things to try and assimilate into whiteness; or, rather, into the version of the girl I thought the boy I liked might date in my middle and early high school years. I wanted so desperately to be different, to be "better," that I began reevaluating who I was with and who I wanted to be. I wore the same name-brand clothes as the girls he dated did, and I restricted my meals, hoping for a semblance of some control over my body. I struck up odd conversation with him when I could and pretended to find his jokes funny. By my junior year in high school I was over it, though, tired of trying to win the heart of a boy who simply didn't see me that way. I kept the music because I liked it and I liked how good it felt to know music that seemed to understand me the way that I longed for another human being to. I decided to cut everything else I associated with him out of my life, because it was time to look forward and let him go. One person can be embarrassed by an unrequited crush only so many times before she takes the loss and leaves.

Human beings are works in progress, and I am constantly working at happiness, at dreams, at goals, at myself, and I do all the work with a musical soundtrack. There was a mixtape made for me for my first two semesters in college, which I'll listen to again once I remember where it is because I am a sucker for nostalgia. I made a playlist two nights before college graduation loaded with songs like "So Good" by Destiny's Child, "The Way" by Ariana Grande, and "Sweater Weather" by the Neighbourhood. There have been many milestone playlists in my life, but none more important than the one I made for this book. Artists include: Stevie Wonder, Carly Rae Jepsen, Paramore, and Demi Lovato, of course, and also Beyoncé, Lizzo, SZA, Usher, and others. There were emotions I was trying to make sure I captured for each essay, and the music was vital to the process, as it often is with anything I do.

The capturing of emotions is important for me as a writer and journalist. When I talk to people about the projects they are doing or the characters they are playing, the conversations invariably lead to the distribution of emotion and the way we use emotion to tell stories and to share ourselves with other people. The same thing can be said for concerts, which is why I love them so much. I am a black disabled woman who believes in a God, a higher power who is all-knowing and creating. I believe in God and the ability for concerts to feel akin to a religious experience. I say as much without an ounce of disrespect to the God that I believe in, but in acknowledgment that there has been a moment at every concert when I look around and the music stops, the crowd is singing in unison with the artist on the stage, and I feel like I am being lifted spiritually, like I can see the world more clearly with these strangers who in this moment love what I love and know what I know, and that is that in those moments, singing those lyrics, we are where and who we should be, connected by a group of people or a person who may not know our names but who has touched our hearts and souls, and here we are together thanking her, him, or them with our voices, mine loudly and off-key, but necessary nevertheless.

The way that I enjoy music now is not the same way that I did in that blue station wagon all those years ago. So much of music is consumed digitally; long gone are the cassette tapes. So much of the music finds its home on our phones with streaming services like Apple Music, Spotify, Pandora, and Tidal. The streaming services are great for the amount of music they hold and the wide-ranging genres for any mood, old and new, that you can find. As an Apple Music girl myself, I understand the convenience of songs at your fingertips, but I am also a fan of tradition. Ashley and I trade Demi Lovato CDs. When she releases new music, we get them as gifts for the person with the birthday closest to the release date. I have seen Demi in concert three times with Ashley and Paramore once. There were also the

Backstreet Boys and Gavin DeGraw concerts, because concerts are sort of our thing, a way that we continue to connect with each other even as we continue to grow as individuals. Concerts are another aspect of our friendship that has made us closer and another way in which we agree that music is very much a singular and a collaborative experience. We share the music we love with each other and commiserate about the songs or artists we don't, while knowing that, in either situation, the impact of music is one we will always cherish.

For me, music has meant much more than a string of chords and beautiful vocals. Those things matter, for sure, but they aren't the reason I love it so much. With music I am very selfish, because my love for it was born out of a selfish need to feel understood and like I belonged to a place or a thing like a song. I have found myself in melodies, in notes and chord changes, in a line of lyrics, or an acoustic cover more often than not. During my freshman year of college, as a gift for my birthday, my friend Jenny Cerne sang "Still Hurting" from *The Last Five Years* in one of our university's practice rooms, and my life was forever changed. I became obsessed with the musical, and for years afterward, I'd watch YouTube covers of the song, desperate to find one that moved me the way that Jenny's had. The search was long and tedious, but I eventually found a soundcheck cover by Lea Salonga that she did in 2016 and another rendition sung by Cynthia Erivo also in 2016. I listen to both at least once every few months, though I wish I had recorded Jenny's version secretly all those years ago, because I can't get her to sing it for me again. Maybe this book will inspire her. *The Last Five Years* means as much to me as *Wicked*, *Hairspray*, and *The Color Purple* and one billion other musicals I love but have not had the chance to see live. Sure, the vocals are amazing and the performances breathtaking, but the true importance is in the message behind the shows.

Music, regardless of genre, harnesses its magic in the messaging. On Broadway, the productions are big and grand with massive audiences to entertain, while your average musician or group, Beyoncé aside, are tasked only with that tall order at concerts. The rest of the time the experience of their singles and albums is an individual one. When you come together with friends and strangers to hear the singles and albums, you are doing so under the assumption that you will not hear or feel exactly what the person next to you is hearing or feeling but instead will come away with an understanding that the thing you are experiencing together is special in both its individualism and collectiveness.

Like most people, unless I am trying to fall asleep, silence makes me uncomfortable. The discomfort comes from years of trying to block my mind and its negative thoughts, and failing repeatedly. We spend so much time with ourselves, and when you are recovering from self-hating tendencies, time alone and with silence is not always the safest place to be, but when you have tasks to complete and music to listen to, it is easier to manage. Music was my way of expressing how I felt without having to say the words. However, as with all things before I began working at happiness, I am figuring out the ways in which I communicate with music as I look to grow as a person who cares about her own health and well-being while making sure that I do not fall back into old thought patterns. The act of transformation with regard to music is an often-explored topic; nevertheless, I have always been mystified by the magic of music, obsessed with people who could sing and infuse music with the magic of hearing it for the first time, every single time. I have become a little obsessive with the type of people who reflect my emotions and thoughts back to me, the people who seem to understand how meaningful it is to be stirred in that way. My mother has and her mother had beautiful singing voices—my mother said once that to hear my grandmother sing with her siblings was akin to a live concert in your own home, in the way that they just knew which notes to hit and when. I wish I could have heard it, too. I would've held on to that memory in an effort to keep my grandmother and her siblings for much longer than I was able to. Whenever I see the sun I think of my grandmother, but whenever I listen to a song she loved I feel her, and that makes being without her slightly easier.

One of the first things life will teach you when you are desperate for better, for more, for some semblance of understanding of who you were and who you want to be, is that anything worth having takes work. The making of a person does not happen overnight, in the same way that the making of music does not happen overnight, and not without the hardships and changes along the way. Music is in everything we consume in one way or the other, and it has held me together when I would have fallen apart. It has given me relief from myself and a place to be with myself. What else can be there for the best and worst versions of yourself and remain good the entire time? I cannot think of any other things, and that is part of the reason music will always be an important part of my past, present, future, and recovery. How do you thank the musicians who have helped you become a better person through the art they created in part to heal themselves? I can't say that I have a concrete answer, but I hope that this suffices.

CRY, BABY, CRY

I cried a lot as a baby. I cried so often that most of my pictures are just of me crying in various places: at birthday parties, in portrait studios, at home on couches and floors, at McDonald's before and after cake, on field trips, and at school. There are other places, but they would take forever to list here, so I am going to assume you get the picture. Crying was easy and free, messy but familiar. I understood the power that came with tears long before I understood the power I wielded outside of them. We were like old friends, long before I understood what a friendship was. In the 1990 movie *Cry-Baby*, starring Johnny Depp as the title character, a young "good" girl falls in love with a juvenile delinquent. At least, that's what I can remember. The movie is quite weird, and I still do not completely understand it, but I remember the prim-and-proper girl crying into a jar and later drinking her own tears when she is kept from seeing Cry-Baby. I also understood that the juxtaposition of masculinity against Cry-Baby's tears was important to note, even as a child who proudly wore her tears. I had the privilege to do so, the expectation that if I did, it wasn't something that would cause alarm. So I cried as often as I felt necessary. (I think the phrasing for that is "a colicky baby"? Though I am not sure I fit that bill, because in my family we never called it that.

I was just a baby who cried like it was my favorite thing to do, and my family, to their neverending credit, loved me anyway and as is.) I often feel stings of regret because I don't have many pictures of myself as a child, simply because I refused to relent until about age four. I lost out on the preservation of time because I couldn't keep still, and like many people, I tended to harp on the things that I couldn't change and wish for do-overs that were possible only in the movies.

It's funny to realize later how in touch and unapologetic we are with our emotions as kids. The ease of expression, the lack of care or consciousness of how we look to others. I miss that a lot more now than I expected to. We lose that sense of confidence far too early, I think. Maybe that's why it is almost always impossible to remember the fearlessness with the same clarity that we can remember the song lyrics and shows we once loved from that same period. I remember my own fearlessness vaguely yet deeply enough to know that it was brief, cut short at the hands of someone who showed me how the world saw me but who was just a child trying to live in the world, too: Jackson.

Leah hardly ever cried when we were kids; I think I took her tears in some kind of negotiation within the womb. I like to think of us as if we were sitting across a table from each other, dividing up duties and plans for when we would enter the world outside our mother's body. We'd spend our in utero days negotiating our emotional responses to the world at large and to each other. I would go on to do most of the talking in our earliest years, anyway. If Leah did cry it was because of something I did, whether it was biting or digging her skin when we fought. She was the balance, my nearly complete opposite. After all, we couldn't both be the crying baby; we had to choose, and I chose to partake in what I believe to be the performance art of crying. An actress at heart, I cried and cried openly even if I was too young to remember it later. But I know that crying was what I was known for as a child—that is, until the day I learned that crying was categorized as a show of weakness. The weakness was packaged as unattractiveness: an emotional girl was "too much" for a guy to want to handle. We were socialized by our peers and our culture at large to "toughen up," to never be the girl a guy wanted to call "crazy." I cried only when necessary: in the dark of rooms with closed doors and shattered hearts and on the couches of close friends after letting too much hurt stack itself inside me like Jenga pieces.

So much of the act of crying during my early childhood centered on physical pain. The physical pain came from things as simple as falls after I tripped over air, untied shoelaces, and accidentally being pricked with sticks if I was outdoors playing. I fell a lot as a kid. I don't fall as often now, but the effect of falls on my body has always been harsh. Sometimes my body hurts for no reason at all, stinging and aching from the push and pull of my muscles and joints. There was also the physical pain behind the recovery that was required postsurgeries. There was the time in middle school when I fell on the way to Girl Scouts and had a concussion that left me unaware of the fact that I had called one of my teachers my aunt and spoken incoherently. Or the time after cheerleading practice when I was tackled by an overexcited boy during a game of touch football. I didn't necessarily fear these moments or the later consequences of my injuries. I had little understanding of fragility. I just navigated the world doing what I pleased until I fell somewhere due to poor coordination or the pain meds wore off, and then I felt the pain I hadn't anticipated. Then that pain stopped, and I was back at my life again, too aloof or fearless to remember the way my body lived with pain.

In the years before I turned twelve, I thought physical pain was the only real reason to cry, because I was too haplessly happy to hurt in any other way. But after age twelve, when I learned just how my body was viewed and took up space in the eyes of non–family members and acquaintances, I retreated within myself. The only way I allowed myself the room to release the feelings that I could not yet name was through the addition of the physical pain, which had always acted as an emotional catalyst. I may not have quite understood the emotional pain, but physical pain was easy to place and understand, the aching hips, hamstrings, legs, and heel cords all too familiar. The stinging legs from the slaps of my own hand in frustration when I failed to do a seemingly simple task. The self-inflicted and involuntary pain hurt like hell, yet at least I knew that my tears for that pain were "justifiable."

My family understood that three surgeries at once was a lot for a young girl or anyone at all to take on. I was fourteen when the three-for-one surgery took place at Shriners Hospital in Pennsylvania. The surgery was tasked with helping me fix my gait so that my hips would even out and I could walk a little straighter. To do this, the team of doctors needed to put a metal plate in my right hip and take tendons from my hamstring and put them in my heel cord. All of this was done in one surgery. I had to relearn how to walk when it was all over, with the understanding that I would go back a year later to have the plate removed. My family rallied around me; they understood the intense physical pain I was under. That was all I wanted them to understand. I didn't understand the emotional pain at that point, so I convinced myself that they didn't, either, that they didn't need to know that I was hurting myself to try and figure it out. Don't get me wrong: I did cry postsurgeries because they hurt like you wouldn't believe, but at the tender age of fourteen, I let more than a few "I hate being in my body" tears fall alongside the others. Still, I knew I had to be strategic, because as a culture we value physical pain in ways we might never value invisible or emotional pain. I already felt like a burden to my family just by existing, despite their unwavering love and support, but if I let them know how I was truly hurting, I thought they might view me differently. Even now, it is so easy for me to worry about my emotions pushing people away, making them see a part of me that they may not like—but I have to risk it.

When you can see something, it allows you to believe it can be fixed via a variety of options—but how can you fix what you can't see? How do you describe the way it shapes who you are becoming without a real idea of why it feels like it is only ever happening to you? I certainly had no idea. So I allowed my tears to fall publicly only when I had the excuse of physical pain and the comfort of knowing it could keep my secrets.

....

The emotional pain–based tears would come later. Not publicly, of course, but privately and with such vigor that it surprised me. Still, I was unable to break the tether of my belief that only visible pain was valid, so I created my own visual aid, lining my body with tiny, barely there cuts. They were deep enough to sting, like paper cuts, because I thought I deserved the pain. They were small enough not to be seen by curious eyes but big enough to satisfy the urge to punish myself. For a long time, they were my excuse to cry, because even if I was the only one I let see them, I felt like I needed to prove to myself that I was allowed this pain and my existence warranted it as well. That is, until I grew tired of the hiding, the extra pain that, even though I thought I deserved it, was still pain at the end of the day. And then there were the Band-Aids, the lies, and the scarring.

The first time I remember crying for an internal pain that was emotional was after a particularly hard day at school. I failed a math test because I have always been terrible with numbers, and I turned that failing grade into concrete proof that I was the world's most unintelligent, ugly, and disappointing person. I cried for the person I'd never be and the grasp on math I'd never have. That day, I cried for every hurt I could not name. In hindsight, it was silly to be so upset about a math test, but it never really was about that. It was about what I believed the failing math grade said in terms of who I was. Indeed, I spent so many of my high school and college years crying for who I was because I was too depressed to see who I could be. Before that failing grade and every one I knew I'd have after it, I realized that this was a reality and a disappointment I would have to learn to manage because it was, in many ways, forever. Later in college, when I passed a math class with a B+ and everyone else got an A+, I celebrated—but we'll get there.

The act of finally allowing myself the room to cry over pain I couldn't see or name felt like beating the hardest level on a favorite game. The release of that pent-up pain for the first time would both help and hurt me in the long run. I felt like I had opened the floodgates, and depression came soon thereafter. In all probability, it had been there before but I hadn't acknowledged it. I found familiarity and comfort in a sadness that greeted me like I belonged only to it and nothing else. In the short run, there was a positive aspect to my pain: it allowed me to acknowledge the worth of a full range of emotion before it settled so deep that it felt never-ending and impossible to manage.

I am still trying to manage my emotions today because, like me, they can get messy and complicated, and life has always been good at throwing curveballs my way. (Even without these curveballs, I have always been a very emotional person. The crying, the doubt and anger, come to me easily.) However, the emotional pain that began my mental illness journey was the result of a wide-ranging list of scenarios I created in my head. As a writer or creative, we do this for a living—create worlds and people that we can't stop thinking about. However, this was different. When we want to hurt ourselves most, we tend to do so with what could've been and what should've been, who we could be versus who we actually are. So, the scenarios in my head that allowed me to cry in the safety of a darkened room often involved boys rejecting me and fear manifesting itself in the form of growing old and dying alone, among other things like whether my friends hated me or I'd said something too loudly in class. I combed through every mistake I had ever made in these scenarios, mistakes that had changed the course of real-life conversations and broken my heart. It is a different kind of beast to spend so much time with your thoughts that you create a whole new life that you are convinced is better in every way than the one you are living.

I know that this sounds a lot like the premise of *Coraline*, in which a bored girl feels neglected until she finds a secret doorway to an alternate version of her life, but I hadn't seen the movie until long after I was already imagining a different version of me with a different life, during which I was unable to see the cracks in the idea of perfection. For the most part, the person I was in my idealizations was who I wanted to be in my real life, and I would leave those idealizations angry about not being the bolder and cooler version of myself that my head had created. That's the powerful thing about our minds: they can allow us to hurt ourselves in ways that seem unimaginable until we are in the thick of our thinking. No one hurt me like I hurt myself, yet I thought that was going to be what saved me and prepared me for a world that was going to. I would carry this idea well into adulthood, as we sometimes do with the harmful practices we teach ourselves as kids yet do not recognize as harmful.

I would adopt some more unhealthy practices around the intricacies of crying and shame that I still can't quite shake, in part because comfort, even in the form of bad habits, still feels familiar enough not to want to abandon. Especially when you can be as stubborn as I can.

....

Crying is only one physical act of emotion, but it has been central to my life for twenty-seven years mostly because I both want and need it to be. Crying is beautiful and it allows me the room to be all that I am even in the midst of turmoil and doubt, and to still see my own worth. It is one of the few acts that every single person on this earth, regardless of race and ethnicity, ability, socioeconomic status, sexual orientation, religion, or what have you, can and will experience, and even the people who have to use artificial tears understand the feeling and necessity behind the act and art of crying and letting yourself just be in it for a healthy amount of time. I have spent so much of my life searching for explanations to my feelings and emotions. I am often fixated on naming them so that they can then be sorted and put away, as to not inconvenience my loved ones.

Aside from crying itself, feelings in general did and do scare me, but I feel so strongly still. I'd love to sit here and tell you that feelings don't have this effect anymore, but I don't feel like lying. What I've learned, though, is that we have feelings whether we want to or not, but expressing them is a beast of a different form and a necessary one. For a baby who loved to cry in public, I became a woman who tried her best to cry in secret, tucking away the hurt to try and tend to it on her own so that she did not become a burden to others. I know now that I was not, nor will I ever be, a burden to others. I am a human being first, whom people love in part because I am in touch with my emotions and aware of how they serve the relationships in my life. In living a life of shame with regard to my emotions, I grew tired and weary. I said and did things that were so outside who I know myself to be that with each outburst, each verbal shot I took, I felt like I was watching it happen outside my body, and so intervening and stopping myself in the moment never felt possible. After losing the friendship of my first college roommate, I saw the damage I was doing and wanted it to end, so I knew that I needed to make some changes in the way I approached my emotions as well as the people in my life.

I started the process by listening to songs like "Who You Are" by Jessie J and "I Am" by JoJo. I know that sounds cheesy, but hearing other people sing about feeling what they need to feel and finding their worth helped me find mine. Music, honesty, and free-writing allowed me to get on the same page as my emotions, and so did crying when I needed to for whatever reason—without trying to find an excuse I thought would be palatable for those around me. In making that change, I also had to be open to working on my conflict-resolution skills.

In the face of honesty, I am a very ugly crier. For a long time, I tried to perfect the movie cry: controlled tears, the non-red and slightly puffy face, and the ability to pull at the heartstrings of viewers without the running nose, but I was not successful. To spare strangers, I try not to do it in public much, but I will if I have to, because odds are they aren't more concerned with my reasons for crying than the reason for my limp. Many people have assumed that each is a direct result of the other, and they can be. Sometimes I am in so much pain in public spaces, I do cry, but most of the time, I am simply crying from laughing too hard or because I am a sap who becomes overwhelmed by how much she loves the people in her life.

And in crying freely, I have discovered that the more that I cry, the more I discover valid reasons to do so. Before I became in touch with and unashamed of my tears, I only ever cried from physical, emotional, and grief-based pain. Now, though, I can and do cry when I am happy. Happy crying is the best. I find myself so grateful in these moments. When I saw the movie *Love, Simon* with Ashley, I cried like six times because I was so happy for Simon (Nick Robinson) and Bram (Keiynan Lonsdale) to have found each other. I also cried after *Black Panther* because to see an almost all-black cast shine on the big screen in such a regal and unapologetic way, and being directed by a black man, moved me. In the same way, I cried while watching *A Wrinkle in Time.* Relatedly, I cry whenever Oprah gives a rallying speech, and I do not apologize for it.

My friends call me their sap because I can literally be sitting on my couch and feel myself tearing up just thinking about how grateful I am for them—so then I have to text them and tell them about it. I have had so many reasons to cry tears of joy since 2016, when my career took off: major bylines, partnerships with clothing companies, immensely kind emails, dream interviews, public speeches, and kind gifts from friends, family, and strangers. I cry when my niece says "I love you, Titi Keah" when we are just sitting on the couch watching TV or listening to music she likes on my phone and bopping our heads in time with the beat. I often find myself getting choked up when new music by artists I love is released, because I cannot and will not contain my excitement. I've cried to the pictures of my uncle Scott and grandmother Vera Brown in the kitchen of my home, where they sit in a see-through cabinet and have walked with me in spirit through every part of this book-writing process. I will likely cry again when someone hopefully chooses to love me, but I think it will be a mixture of both joy and relief.

....

The relief crying has happened a few times in my life thus far. I cried in relief and pride at my college graduation—tears that were mixed with a little bit of fear surrounding what might be next for me. I cried one morning after going to bed with heartburn, convinced that it was something mysterious and deadly, only to wake up the next morning completely fine and with the kind of new lease on life that comes from a night of panic and WebMD searches. (I did say I could be quite dramatic.) When it comes to food, I have teared up at the sheer goodness of the right dish in the right restaurant after forgetting to eat before any point in that day.

The heaving kind of ugly relief cry happened for me when my aunt Regina ("Gina") found out she had cancer after having lost a large amount of weight quickly and for seemingly no reason at all. Since I had lost my uncle Scott to a rare form of cancer unexpectedly, I was sobbing unabashedly in the Roswell hospital waiting room, petrified that we would lose her, too. I prayed pretty much nonstop between her first tests and her last, before we knew what was going on. I cried myself to sleep for weeks worrying about her, but the doctors had caught her cancer early and were able to stop it from spreading. Due to the early diagnosis, a chemo pill regimen, and weekly shots of iron, my aunt is alive today, and I cry a little with relief every time I stop and think about it. She is my favorite person to celebrate wins with at the casino, and the person who helped me cultivate my love for books early as a child. Admittedly she and I butt heads from time to time, but at the end of the day, I love her with all my heart. I love all my aunts, Renee and Michele and my aunt-in-law, Michelle, and I know that they, too, are people I can go to with tears for any reason.

Sometimes I catch myself crying out of pure relief in the small moments when I am reminded that I matter to my people because they want me to, not because I have to. I spend a lot of time grateful for being wanted and chosen, for being comfortable in my skin and in the presence of people who are more attractive than me without seeing it as a personal failure for not being them. In retrospect, that is a huge insecurity of mine, the desire to be valued by people outside my family. All people want to be wanted, to be shown they matter, and in having that I allowed myself to have joy through emotion as well. Growth is often the catalyst of my happy tears. I am very proud of who I am becoming and respectful of who I was, aside from a few self-deprecating jokes here and there. The reality of my life is that now many of my reasons for crying are mixed. I am not just doom and gloom or happy and relieved. I am multifaceted in the way I have always longed to be, both bold and brave, soft and hard, beautiful in my own way. In the same way that we are never just one thing, neither are our emotions or the reasons behind them.

There are also the tears as a result of being alive—because I *want* to be alive now. This is new territory, exciting territory, a place I don't mind being in for a longer period. I think this is the case because I learned how to embrace not only my body but also my life in a way I had not before. My tears were the result of my pain just for being, but now they are a testament to how good life can be with both good and bad days and a lot of effort.

In learning to embrace my feelings, I learned to celebrate the small things, too, like meditating in the morning, walking longer distances, arriving places on time or early, and surprising my friends with just-because gifts. Without tears like that B+ final exam math grade that affirmed growth for me, the bigger-occasion tears would not feel as good. I silently celebrate trips to the store

or the ice cream shop with my mom and Leah, and I publicly acknowledge compliments about my writing and clothing because I
believe that marginalized people in particular are expected to do so
much quietly and without acknowledging the work that has gone
into the thing we are being complimented on. I am not doing that;
I have worked too hard and spent too much time trying to dim my
light so others could shine. My emotions and I are over that, and
we will be loud and proud. Celebrating smaller and bigger wins is
imperative in being unapologetic, and it is also fun, because we
should all be proud of the work we do. It doesn't hurt anyone to
acknowledge the people who appreciate the work we do. I also celebrate getting up and putting clothes on even though I often write
from home and do not need to, but I do anyway because it really
does improve my mental health.

When I was younger I heard a lot of people talk about not in-
dulging in the small victories, but I do because they matter, too.
When I catch myself in the midst of doing small things that bring me
joy, I do a little happy dance and remember that being kinder to myself costs me nothing. The small stuff leads to medium celebrations
and then the big ones. We owe it to ourselves to celebrate and feel it
all, so that when the moment fades, the memory never will. In the
world we are currently living in, acknowledging our feelings helps
us be better not only to ourselves but also to other people, because
empathy is possible only when you can first recognize it in yourself.
(This is not to dismiss the struggles of people who have neurological
issues such that they can't do so.) When I think about all the loss
surrounding us in the world and in my own—the loss of high school
classmates before our ten-year high school reunion, those with so
much ahead of them—my chest tightens at the thought of who these
people never got the chance to be. There is the loss of innocence

and the belief that we never have to worry about who we will lose; I think about the way that grief is possible only because we allow ourselves the room to feel, and if we told the people we care about how much they matter to us not only with our words but also with our emotions, we could have the satisfaction of knowing they know how deeply they matter beyond lip service. The thought is idealistic in nature and maybe a little too simple, but I find myself hoping for a world that uses vulnerability as a tool to be more understanding and aware of the power behind emotion.

When we are vulnerable, I believe that we are our truest selves. Emotion is all about vulnerability, and that is why, in the cheesiest sense, it is so beautiful. What an honor it is to have people you can be your truest and most open self with, as well as to have the ability to be that person for yourself, to recognize that no matter what hurts or who hurts you, you deserve healing, you deserve a life that you can enjoy and be comfortable in. Vulnerability feels like one of the keys to that life. We are vulnerable when we are young because we don't know not to be. As children, we see the world as a place for us to be whoever we want to be, and we allow ourselves the freedom to scream and cry because we still consider those things valid forms of communication. But we lose that as we age, for a variety of reasons. We are conditioned and socialized to grow into teenagers who then become adults who decide that emotion, particularly crying, is the enemy to success. If we took the stigma away from "inconvenient" or visible emotion, if we stopped conditioning ourselves to tuck or hide away the messier parts of life, maybe we'd all have reason to cry happy tears and understand happiness in a way that we haven't before. Given our current political climate, those of us in danger of having our rights being taken away have only our voices and each other with which to make positive change. Allowing the space for emotion will also allow us to keep fighting even when everything feels hopeless, even if and when we are knocked down.

As we long for what we do not have, we tend to withhold from ourselves what we know to be important, because we believe that the sacrifice will get us where we want to be. Imagine if we didn't. Imagine if we gave ourselves the same sort of love, attention, and understanding we give the people we love. If we allowed our vulnerability to fuel us to be better people, to say and do more, to feel in and navigate a world that champions tears as much as it does strength, to see tears and crying as signs of strength, even. Or if we lived in a world that let people live their lives and didn't judge them for crying—because if anyone should understand how hard the world can be to live in, it should be the other inhabitants of that world. I want us to have the ability to open ourselves up in a world that gives a damn about the other people in it whether or not they look like us, share our sexual orientation, or have our same abilities. At the risk of sounding like an after-school special, I can say that crying, for a variety of reasons, has made me a better person, a happier and more fully realized person, in ways that nothing else has.

....

I think a lot about how we don't often give ourselves the room to be sad, to say we are hurting. Often for marginalized people of color, our sadness is misinterpreted as anger, whether the tears are streaming down our face or not. That misinterpretation can lead to physical harm and even death. So for us to be emotional, to show our sadness, is a revolutionary act, because we don't know how other people may respond, even those closest to us. When I rediscovered my love for the song "Everything" by Fefe Dobson, I thought first about how we failed her and didn't make her the star she deserved to be. But then

I realized that two lines of the song are perfect for explaining the pride in feeling whatever emotions we want while still expecting to be respected and loved with them anyway: "Sometimes I won't / Give in to you." The chorus continues the theme. I love the idea of laying all of your cards out on the table and saying, "Love me for all that I am or I am done, I refuse to keep waiting and trying to be anything but who I am comfortable being." Getting in touch with our emotions is hard—looking in the mirror and sitting with the reality of the person looking back at you can be. The work isn't easy, because our emotions are attached to how we view ourselves and how the world in turn may view us as a result of sexism, racism, homophobia, transphobia, and systemic oppression. Still, our emotions are often something we are self-conscious about due to conditioning by our society. Imagine for a moment that there wasn't that pressure to be aspects of stereotypical ideas of marginalized communities: to be stoic and proud, strong and sure, to make the sacrifice of putting everyone above yourself all the time without acknowledging your own emotions. Imagine if we took the time to get in touch with our emotions enough to cry when we needed for whatever reason, without the resulting shame or anger? It feels possible, but first we have to reckon with and learn to love all parts of who we are so that we do not care about the people who stare or have something to say about the way that we live our lives.

After being taught these ideas from all sides, from the oppressors and the oppressed, from the people who do not like you and the people who love you, any one person would question if the backlash against change is worth it. There is an extra bit of sting when you remember how the people you love and who love you can hurt you in ways neither of you can recognize until after the fact. Often, the harmful things we place on people we care for were placed on us. That is why we have to forgo excuses and do the work of correcting those learned behaviors so that we do not continue a terrible cycle.

For marginalized people of color there is also the insistence that we pray about our hurt and pain and bottle up our emotions because all healing can be found through religion. I don't believe this advice is always given with ill intentions, but it is often given because it is all that the people giving it were allowed to do when they turned to someone they trusted with their own hurt or when they were looking for ways to deal with their own pain. The truth is that it doesn't make it okay. I am in no way making excuses for toxic and harmful ideologies around emotional expression and mental health. I do, however, think the acknowledgment of a reasoning behind these behaviors and practices allows us to understand a pattern built by oppression that trickles all the way down to our own unique experiences of emotion, which leads us to avoid things that can truly help us, such as counseling.

The fact of the matter is that things like going to counseling and being open to my friends about my emotions, even if that means screaming one good time at the top of my lungs, laughing loudly, or crying until my voice is hoarse, has saved my life, saved me from further harming myself, or passing on destructive ideologies to the people whom I know and love who trust me enough with the hurt and pain of their own.

Times are finally changing, along with attitudes, but there is still work to be done. With shifts in culture and ideology needing to start at home and in our own relationships, in order to change the culture we have to start small. We need to end both the practice of suppressing our emotions for fear of judgment and the stigma attached to crying, too. As a child and young girl, I cried when something was and wasn't wrong, though I didn't have a way of knowing what was and wasn't wrong in my mind and tear ducts at that age. As silly as it is, I wish I had, so I could now give my family members an explanation and an apology for being so hard to deal with. I want this even though I understand the irony in this wish, the need to please even when I know that I know better. I am imperfect and learning along the way.

My favorite thing about crying is that it is messy and complicated in the same way that life can be. As human beings we can't just wrap our emotions up in a nice bow, and I think that's what makes life so exciting: we don't know what will happen next, but our bodies will figure out a way to react regardless. Our bodies, minds, and hearts deserve to react the way they see fit, and in return, we should be able to channel these reactions into a healthy and cathartic expression. When I think about all the tears I have shed in my life, I smile. I smile not because they were fun, easy, or exciting. I smile because, like the other seemingly inconsequential things in my life, I am not sure who I would truly be if I had not tapped into my emotions in this way. I don't know if I'd be here now or would actually like the person I would have become without first having an immense urge to cry, then being ashamed of my tears later, and finally finding a healthy balance when it truly counted.

TO SEE AND BE SEEN

The first people who saw and who still see me completely do not look like me, yet they saw me long before I saw myself. They are mostly able-bodied, black, brown, and white. Some of the people are related to me, but most of them are not. Indeed, I have two families—the one I have chosen and the one I was born into. I consider that a very lucky circumstance in my life, the joy of being understood and cared for by a plethora of people who do and don't look like me. I have spent a lot of my life trying to go unnoticed and feeding into the idea of my being a nuisance with the aid of a body that was different and therefore strange. Nevertheless, through this desire to fly under the radar, I have been loved and discovered, nurtured and molded into a person who understands her worth and the loneliness of invisibility, the isolation of the "fine on my own" ideology. The process of opening myself up to the people in my world leads to the power of visibility. This is what love can do.

We don't talk about platonic love enough, how necessary and fulfilling it is. The love of my friends and family has sustained me when not much else could. I believe that it is possible to be in love with your friends without its being romantic. I also know how heartbreaking it can be when we lose platonic love. But I never really thought about the power of platonic love until I lost it for the first time. I was in my freshman year of college and my roommate (let's call her Sarah) was the kind of friend I longed for. She was smart, funny, kind, and she liked me. I had friends long before her, but with most of them, it seemed that they liked me out of obligation or convenience. I lacked the self-worth to trust in the personal choices my friends made when they chose me. Sarah, as well as the other five close friends I would meet my freshman year and the entirety of college, liked me but didn't have to, I thought. I am not the same person I was my freshman year of college, thank God; I was clingy and mean then, scared of disappointing people and convinced that the only way to keep myself from being hurt was to hurt them first when the opportunity presented itself. Sarah, rightfully so, had enough after a while, and though I believe we had genuinely good times, I became too much. Sarah wanted to move back home to be closer to her mother, and despite not having the right to object so vehemently, I did. The last conversation we ever had was on Facebook. I tried to use my grandmother's death to justify my clinginess and subsequent anger at Sarah for choosing to go home and changing another thing in my life instead of staying at our university with me. In our last conversation, Sarah expressed sympathy for my grief but explained the ways in which I had hurt her and that she did not want to be friends anymore. I cried in secret for the four days that followed because I knew that she was right. I was the toxicity in our relationship. I would spend a few years begging for forgiveness that I did not deserve. Her resounding silence was punishment enough.

We are still friends on Facebook despite not being in each other's lives. I hid her from my newsfeed but I go to her profile from time to time. She seems happy, and that makes me happy because even though she will never know who I am now, I will never forget who she was to me or who we were to each other before our friendship imploded. The loss of that friendship would have a great impact on me for the following year and a half. I cried to my college counselor with worry that the other friends would leave me one day, too. I cried because I believed I was worthless and because Sarah really was gone out of my life and there was nothing I could do to win her back. In order to understand the pain inflicted on me by others, I had to face the pain I caused. There was the pain I caused Leah, both physical and emotional for years until college, and the pain I caused Sarah by expecting her to drop her every other life responsibility to stay with me at our particular college because I didn't like change; and then, when she did not, I cared more about my anger and feelings of resentment than her need to do what was best for her. Sometimes you can be the toxic person in someone's life even in your quest to be seen and understood, and you can hurt someone in your quest to heal yourself. I certainly did. Sarah and I do not speak anymore, but I apologized constantly after everything went down, only realizing that my desire for forgiveness had more to do with my guilt than it did with being apologetic. It took me a full year to understand just how I had hurt her, and the realization to lead me to be genuinely sorry for the pain I had inflicted on her. By then, though, I realized that by constantly asking for her forgiveness I was only harming her. She didn't owe me anything but I owed her a complete separation from me. We had great times before the end of our friendship: she saw me though my mood swings and endured my well-honed sarcasm, but we no longer know each other. Sarah saw me but she does not see me anymore, and still I look on the time we were friends with fondness because it was beautiful for what it was, even if it will never be again. In truth, I have hurt many of the people who have chosen to see me fully and love me anyway in some way or the other with my words or actions. The reason that they are still in my life or have forgiven me is because I have thankfully matured. I have learned to handle my fears and disagreements with the grace and care I did not have before. In many ways, my friendship with Sarah was a lesson in what not to do to the people who see me and love me still.

My five other closest friends did not end our friendships, though there were times in our four years of college when I deserved as much. We played cards on weekends with Dragon Berry rum and ginger ale, quoted the song from the movie *The Hangover* about best friends, laughed about a *Mad TV* skit about getting an order wrong at a fast food place, and sang songs we knew only the choruses to. Me, a black woman, let five white women into my life and they became forever friends, despite our different navigations of the world and identities. We watched *Glee* in different dorm rooms each week and made time for *Pretty Little Liars*, too. We made small moments count despite how busy our schedules and majors made us; we made time for each other like Lena, Tibby, Bee, and Carmen in *The Sisterhood of the Traveling Pants*. In fact, I am still very close to four of these friends today. I took pictures with the Sanderson sisters at Jenny's Halloween wedding in 2015, drank wine and played cards with Leigh in 2017, stood beside Tinni at Felicia Kazmierczak née Rivera's wedding in 2017, and won several games of Phase 10 on mobile against Tinni in 2018. All before Felicia, Leigh, and I packed our bags and got in Felicia's car to drive three and a half hours to visit Tinni in September 2018. We don't see each other every single day anymore, but we try our best to make sure that we talk at least once a week on the phone, via text message, or during a multiplayer game on our phones. These women were my first away-from-home friends. We weathered the fear, excitement, and frustration of college together. We laughed, cried, and laughed some more while figuring ourselves out and learning about life and each other. I love these women now and I will love them forever because they gave me a chance to be better and to be loved by a group of people who loved me back even though we were not blood related. Before them, though, there were and are other platonic loves of my life.

....

I met my best friend, Ashley Allcorn, at the tail end of my senior year in high school, which was our second semester. I introduced myself to her in a public speaking class by saying, "Hi, I'm Keah, we're going to be best friends." I did so because I loved the "Who Am I?" speech she gave a week late because she came into the class a week after it began. I also told her we would be best friends because of the *Kim Possible* card she used for one of her visual aids as representation of one of her favorite childhood shows. Ashley is one year younger than I am, and while I was away at college, we grew closer, texting every day and hanging out when I was home on breaks. Throughout all four years of college, through friend breakups, the death of my grandmother, and the ups and downs, I knew I would be okay because I had Ashley in my corner. When Ashley was moving to California in 2015, we took a trip to Target for last-minute things she needed before leaving in the morning. I was worried that the distance would end our friendship when I hugged her goodbye that night and smiled through watery eyes. However, the distance has only strengthened our friendship. We text every single day and call on weekends. We plan what we will do when I visit her, which will likely include eating the pinwheel sandwiches that I loved when her mom first made them for us in high school, watching movies we adore, and drinking alcohol. The last time that I saw her was particularly emotional: it was in January 2017, the day after Donald Trump was sworn into office. I'd flown to California for a conference, and she drove two hours to see me the following day.

When we are apart, we catch each other up on the weekly happenings of our lives and complain to each other about TV shows that the other person may not even watch. Ashley is the second best friend I have ever had in my life, but we work toward making our friendship work in a way I did not know how to the first time I had a best friend. She is the first person I turn to when I am having a good or difficult day. I call her mother "Mama H." because I consider her my second mom and her last name starts with an *H*. And Ashley's brother, Nigel, I consider my younger brother, too. Together, they are all my second family. They welcomed me into their lives with open arms and open hearts. Ashley and I care too much about the friendship we've built to let it falter, and as twentysomethings trying to figure out the world and where we fit, our friendship is a constant that has strengthened our resolve on our worst days and cheered us on during our good ones. A running aspect of our friendship has always been that she is Meredith Grey and I am Cristina Yang from *Grey's Anatomy*, both strong, smart, and funny with great taste in clothes. We have each other's backs in the same way they do, too. She is Meredith in her ability to calm me down and keep me sane. I am Cristina most when I say and mean that she is my person and she makes me brave.

Technology has enhanced my friendships and has allowed me to feel seen and understood. For example, Erica Wrobel and I met in college but became close only afterward. She lives in California, too, so our friendship spans over three thousand miles and is aided by technology to keep us connected when we can't be face-to-face. I can talk to her about all things entertainment, Matthew Gray Gubler, podcasts, our favorite writers, and our hopes for our professional and personal futures. One of my oldest friends whom I met when we were in middle school, Lorraine, I communicate with exclusively through phone because she lives in Indiana with her children. I am particularly thankful for the technology of cars, not just for their ability to get me places, but because they are where I dance with one of my other best friends, Stephanie, at red lights. Cars are where we sing along loudly to our favorite songs on Friday nights on the way to Walmart or to get food. I often see Stephanie only once every few weeks, but when we are in her car, singing along to the songs we love, it feels like these moments will last forever, and even when they reach their end, we know there will be more to look forward to as I close her door and walk inside my house.

Throughout the course of our friendship, I've spent a lot of time in Demetrius's car as well. He drags me to events he is invited to and forces me to be social when he knows I need to be. We've been friends for a very long time, and as with many of my friendships, we spend a lot of our time eating and talking, taking a lot of pictures together, and laughing at the silliest things. In some ways, we are polar opposites. He loves to be out and social, constantly doing things and taking trips with his friends, whereas I am a homebody and prefer to stay in. But where we meet in the middle is that we always have a good time together no matter what we are doing. We can sit around playing Cards Against Humanity at his dining room table with my sister and their friends, having a nineties throwback party in his backyard, eating lunch at a local sandwich shop, or spending a Friday night at a hookah bar. Every single time we are together, we know that it is time well spent.

These friends I have met first in real life, but there are others I love just as much whom I have met through the powers of social media. Danielle Sepulveres is my favorite person. (No, really, it's what I call her.) She's beautiful, funny, whip-smart, and kind. I can go to her for any- and everything, and I truly believe she saw me before I saw myself and my potential as a writer. When I did see myself truly for the first time, I knew that I was seeing who she truly saw, and being the person that Danielle truly sees feels at once exciting and like I should've known all along that I was that person.

WhatsApp is where my friendship with Catherine and Amanda flourishes. There we talk about everything and anything. We talk about music, movies, TV shows, and life. They are the first people I go to when I need a reminder that the world is good, that people are worth the effort. We send videos and voice notes to each other that are both lighthearted and heavy in nature. There is a trust that was earned and understood quickly; we lift each other up and champion our successes and encourage each other to keep going during our losses. In this space of three proud black women, we have made a few promises to each other. We have made promises to share joy, links to good music, articles about the things we enjoy, things that remind us of each other and the group chat dynamic. The biggest promise we made is a promise to say what we mean and mean what we say, and so the distance from western New York to Rhode Island to New Orleans doesn't feel so vast at all.

My dear friend Esmé, whom I call my queen because she is regal, her soul is warm and kind, and she is simply a person who radiates grace, and Brandon, who is B!, I met through Twitter. They are honest and talented, they hold me accountable and offer me unwavering support, and they believe in me and my work in a way that I never expected anyone outside my family to. They make me want to be a better writer and person.

Vilissa, Alice, Maysoon, and Rebecca are my sistagirls who have physical disabilities, too. They keep me laughing, sane, and unapologetic in the face of the problems within the disability community. We ride for each other and share opportunities when one of us can't afford to take something else on. They know what it is like to live in a world that wasn't designed with bodies like ours in mind. They also understand what bad days are like, how it is possible to be confident in who you are and still frustrated by the everyday small things that are hard to do like zip up jackets, close doors, grip objects, and navigate public spaces.

The only friend that I was fortunate enough to meet through Twitter offline and in real life so far is my friend Jennifer Pooley. Jennifer is my fairy godmother of sorts. She's introduced me to so many great people, specifically other writers I've long admired like Jodi Picoult, and writers whose work I have read and loved, like Katie Delahanty and Jen Klein. I flew across country to California to attend a writing conference with her. She met me at the airport and we roomed together. She even ran in the rain to get me In-N-Out as a "welcome back to California" gift. I assumed there would be some awkwardness, but there was none. The transition from talking via phone or Twitter to in person was seamless, as though we usually saw each other every single day. We spent the three days of the conference laughing, eating great food, attending great talks, playing Game Night in a Can, and watching Lifetime movies. We watched one unintentionally hilarious movie I can't remember the name of with bad acting where one character shouts the name of her friend Patty before killing her. So now that is how we end most conversations. A funny reminder of the great time we had together and the great times to come. The greatest gift that Jennifer has given me, though, is the gift of calling her my friend, and the gifts of her love, support, and faith in me, faith that I can change the world for the better.

....

My friends made both in real life and online are not the only people who see me for all that I am and love me regardless. (As I mentioned, I am very lucky.) But there is something affirming and beautiful about getting to choose people to love and getting chosen. My chosen family exists in small groups. Each person is very different from the other, but what they all have in common is that their friendship has helped me become a better person who dreams bigger, because I know that even if I fall, I have places to land and people willing to pick me back up. They've allowed me to forgive myself for the years I spent hating myself when they loved me, and, again, for the way I ruined my friendship with Sarah, even when they do not know the full details. I have spent most of my life outside my home in majority-white spaces, and while not all my closest friends are white, most of them are. Although that isn't something I actively sought, every single day I am amazed at the way my shine is never eclipsed by them, as such relationships are often portrayed in popular culture, and that they don't ask me to water down my identities because my pride in them makes them uncomfortable. I appreciate that. My close friends who are black or other people of color—Demetrius, Maysoon, Esmé, Brandon, Vilissa, Alice, Catherine, and Amanda—understand the exhaustion that comes with being multiply marginalized in America. I don't have to explain to them why it hurts so often to look at the news or why laughter is the best medicine and I'd rather sit in joy for a few days and talk only about silly things before it is back to the fight for our rights and livelihood. My friends both white and of color have been instrumental to my growth; we value each other in a way that I never thought I deserved. There is so much power in my love for them because it is built on the strength of our experiences and emotion. My thing has always been to name and claim, so, I name and claim the people in my life, because to name someone you love in the process of your development and healing is to acknowledge that doing it alone was not possible.

Even when I longed for invisibility and what I believed to be the comfort of normalcy, I had the support and love of my blood relatives. In fact, this collection would not have been possible without them. My family and I are very close; it is how we were raised and how we live with a semblance of faith in the world, because we have each other. I have one sister, but my cousins are my "sisters," too: Mykele, Melaine, Kaylee, Meesha, and Mahogony, and my other "brother," my cousin, Jeremy, are all able-bodied but I still find that they know me better than I know myself most days. When we have faced grief we held each other together, letting our bond keep us from feeling alone in any of it. This was most evident in the losses of our grandmother and uncle Scott.

On October 13, 2009, my cousins Mykele and Melaine came home from school and found my grandmother on the living room floor. The paramedics believed that she was heading back from her room when she passed, the house phone in her pocket. At the time, I was seventeen and attending the State University of New York at Fredonia in my first semester of college. There was a scholarship award dinner that weekend, and I was an honoree.

The last conversation my grandmother and I had, on a snowy Thursday night in October, was the only goodbye I ever got, but I was too preoccupied with getting to class on time to recognize it. I pictured her answering the phone, shifting her weight from right to left while she watched an episode of *Stargate SG-1*. She was likely pressed firmly into her chair, glasses on the bridge of her light brown nose, a puzzle book and a pen not too far out of her reach. I made a promise to call her the next day that I didn't keep, and I will forever be angry with myself about that. If I could go back, I would have never let a conversation about a snowstorm and a public speaking class be our last. I would've skipped the class and dropped a grade, wrapping myself in my warmest winter blankets and thanking my grandmother for existing in a world that I didn't yet know could be so cruel. We could've talked about her favorite Westerns and sports teams and yelled at the refs for not doing their jobs. We could've avoided talking about school in favor of talking about her mother. Maybe she could've sung to me the way she used to or asked me if I knew the answer to one of her crossword puzzles. I hate that I will never know what we could've said.

After I got the news of her death, on my used twin bed, pressed against the sole *Twilight* poster on my wall with tears streaming unapologetically down my face, I had never felt farther away from my family, from her, despite being only an hour's drive away. The scholarship award dinner was long forgotten. The walls were closing in as if the air were actually being sucked out of my tiny shared room, as my roommate's paper birds were preparing to fall off her wall again. I wiped my tears and ran across the hall to my friend Leigh. I knocked on her door repeatedly until she answered, falling into her arms before she could ask what was wrong. During my first week of classes just two months earlier, my grandmother had called and

told me that if school ever became too much I could call my uncle
Scott and he would come bring me home, no questions asked. I had
assured her I was fine but still promised to let her know if anything
changed.

I didn't know then that just five years later, at the age of twenty-
three, I would lose my uncle Scott, too. When we got the news that
cancer had taken him just two years shy of fifty with so much more
to do, I was sitting down again. This time, we had just gotten home
from the Roswell hospital believing that we would be able to go back
in the morning to say goodbye. When my aunt Regina—his sister—
called, I was staring at the wall in front of me. The irony wasn't lost
on me that instead of a poster-clad wall that represented my youth
and naïveté about the way grief barges into our lives, an empty wall
save for a clock was staring back at me, an unwanted reminder that
we have so little time with the people we love. He passed away on
August 5, 2014, even though he had promised to walk me down the
aisle whenever the time came, even though there were many more
Father's Day shout-outs to give him on Facebook and even though
I wasn't ready to say goodbye to the man who was the embodiment
of love. I looked to him for so many things, because he was what
strength looked like to me. A man whom everyone loved and wanted
to be around. Once, when he ran me to a doctor's appointment, we
saw six people he knew, and each person had a story about watching
him throw discus in high school, a kind thing he had done for a family member, or a story about how he'd kept them from getting beaten
up. He cared so deeply for people and they cared for him, even if
they hadn't known him for long. They greeted him as if they did, as if
he was each their best friend, the person they looked up to, the way
those of us lucky enough to know him did. Cancer took him before
we could go see another movie or rap another song or say another "I

love you." The last sound that filled my ears that night before sleep finally caught up to me, in the quietest corner of my room, where I sat on another twin bed pressed against a white wall, knees to my chest, was his absence. We have these great memories of the man who helped raise us, helped mold us into the men and women we are today.

My uncle Scott was the best of men. The big, muscled guy with a heart of gold. He did anything and everything for the people he loved, and if he loved you, it was endless. He was the kind of man who stepped up as the positive father figure in my life and in the lives of cousins and siblings when our own fathers did not. He was always ready with a corny old joke that he thought was hilarious or an old-school song, and he was a necessity at parties for a guaranteed good time. Whenever I vented about college, from freshman to senior year, he was the one who gave me the best advice, who believed in me when I couldn't believe in myself. Well before college, when I was still a young girl who believed nothing bad could ever happen to her or the people she loved, he was there for all the monumental moments in my childhood, for when I tried learning how to ride a bike, for every toss in the air that made me feel like I could fly, and for every moment I needed a laugh and a hug.

The thing about death is that while it is unavoidable, it takes more than the person you love. It takes pieces of you, too, leaving only the feeling of absence in its wake. Absence is the thing you will feel on your deceased loved ones' birthdays and on the anniversaries of their deaths, when you ready yourself to remind them of a funny joke they once told and when you call to share good and bad news. You'll feel their absence so completely that it will feel like you're learning they passed for the first time, even years later. I still reach for my phone to call and tell my grandmother good news. I still long for her comforting arms when the world feels too hard to face or the weight of being feels too heavy.

My grandmother and uncle Scott are not here to meet the woman I have become, the happy Keah who loves herself, but a part of me likes to believe that they knew her before they passed, that they knew and saw her coming before I did. My hope is that they know I couldn't have come to her without their love for me first.

....

There is also nothing like a mother's love—or, at least, my mother's love. Cheryl Brown is the perfect one for me. She'll probably scold me when she reads this and sees that I used her name instead of just writing "Mom," but that's a cultural thing. Most black people I know do not refer to their mother, elder aunts, and uncles by their name alone—at least not to their faces—because it is considered disrespectful. So, Mom, I am sorry, love you. My mother was the first person in the world to see me and love me. When the doctors told her I had cerebral palsy, she didn't turn me away or resent me for being different from Leah. She fought for my rights in and out of the classroom, and she loved me like she loved my siblings. The older that I get, the less I think about the things I received as a child. What I remember the most is unwavering love. My mother is funny, beautiful, honest, and confident. I know now that I get these qualities from her. I know now that I could have never learned to love myself without her loving me first and never giving up on me even when I gave up on myself, and even still with every surgery, crying fit, bad mood, and medical complication. I know that not many disabled people can say that they had so many able-bodied people fighting for and loving them the way that I can, and I recognize the luck and privilege in the unconditional love I have received and will receive.

As a disabled black woman, I understand that I am seen and unseen. I am loved by some people and hated by others, because that's the way the world works. Still, so much power is wielded by able-bodied people without chronic illness, people who do not care about disabled people or our community, people who view us as burdens first and people never. That is where I believe the resentment, pain, and anger on the part of the disability community stem from. How do you respect people who are dismissive of you? I have always been a firm believer that respect is earned, not freely given. The history of the harm done to disabled people by able-bodied people without chronic illness or invisible disability cannot simply be forgotten or dismissed. Due to this history, I understand that I am very lucky to be seen and loved by able-bodied people while having to reckon with the fact that there are also able-bodied people who have hurt me and disabled people who have hurt me. Reckoning with that reality is easier when I remember that identity and ability do not save you from pain or from being the cause of pain.

The privilege of being seen by the people who love me allowed me to see myself. To be loved by others when you don't love yourself is a surreal experience, because you don't know why the love is shown to you but you'd give everything to keep it. I never want to give up or take for granted the love I have now.

....

I am still often invisible in the world. When people aren't staring at me in an attempt to figure out what "happened" to my body, they are running into me without apology, trying to walk through me like I am a ghost, and beeping at me from their cars because they think I am walking too slow in the parking lots of stores. In order to best understand this invisibility, imagine the movie *The Princess*

Diaries. In the movie, Mia, played by Anne Hathaway, literally has someone try to sit on her, claiming that he did not see her sitting there. That is how I often feel. Invisibility is an interesting thing to long for until you have it. There was a time when I thought that invisibility was the only way for me to survive in this world, but I was wrong. The moment that I saw the person my friends and family saw, the good with the complicated, was the day that my life truly began. While I do wish for the staring to stop, I no longer want to be invisible to the world or myself. Instead, I will make sure that I am a person people see and know—because I am not an eyesore but a sight for sore eyes.

There is a saying that you can't love someone else before you love yourself, or as RuPaul says, "If you don't love yourself, how in the hell you gonna love somebody else?" I get it, I do, and I hate it because it makes love conditional. However, you see, my grandma Vera and uncle Scott loved me so fiercely and without pause through every tear and rough day and again, through every smile and hug. Yes, all these people loved me before I loved myself, and I turned out better for it. The idea that you must love yourself before anyone else can is a sweet saying in theory, but the love in my life isn't conditional. If I hadn't had these people in my life loving me before and after I loved myself, waiting patiently for me to see what they saw, I do not know if I would've ever gotten around to doing it.

Still, I am not bitter; I am excited to help change the idea of what disability is and isn't, to tell stories where we love and give stories where we live. In seeing myself, I see that there are so many beautiful things and people that are still unseen. The world is still ignoring the fact that disabled people feel and bask in joy. The other side of that is the disability community's decision to ignore or dismiss its members of color, and its gender-nonconforming and LGBTQ+ members, because the truth is that we all have work left to do to make the world a more accepting and inclusionary place. No one is perfect or has all the right answers, but the effort matters, as well as the willingness to better understand and reflect a world wherein no one desires invisibility and no one feels as though she, he, or they are not worthy of being seen and loved. The desire to be seen is not only through eyes, because that is not the only way to see the world. There is touch, as well as traits and characteristics through hearts. From the moment that I understood what love was, I believed that no one could love me, not if they saw me and not if they knew me, but I am loved and I know that despite what the world may think, I am worth loving and seeing.

We must do the work to interrogate whom we see and whom we don't, whom we acknowledge and whom we won't. This work is necessary for global and personal growth. The world should not be so quick to decide that a subgroup holds no value or not enough value to live well in our society the way that everyone deserves. This is not because of the contributions disabled people can make to society, though there are plenty of us who have—like Temple Grandin, Albert Einstein, Harriet Tubman, who, respectively, changed the livestock industry, was one of the most recognizable intellectuals in history, and was a spy and freed more than three hundred slaves. Rather, it's because we are human beings first, who shouldn't have to be inspirations for our lives to matter. Throughout my life thus far, I have looked mostly to able-bodied people without chronic illness for love, comfort, understanding, and trust. For the most part, this is exactly what I have been given by every person and name in this essay. I wasn't given what I hoped and asked for because of my disability or in spite of it; I received all of it because of the person I am inside my body. Again, I am not perfect, as evidenced, but I know for a fact

that it has been a blessing to be cared for by people who do not necessarily look like me and by people who share my skin color but not
my disability. The blessing is so because I have always believed it is
imperative that we learn from the experiences and histories of other
people to better understand each other and ourselves.

I LIKE ME NOW, TOO

I wanted to die. First slowly, and then all at once when I remembered my low threshold for pain. I read the line in the John Green novel *The Fault in Our Stars*, "I fell in love the way you fall asleep: slowly, and then all at once," but I made it about death and what I believed to be the release of torture. I love John Green's books and I doubt my interpretation of a line he wrote was what he intended. Love felt too far from my reality, so I switched it to something that felt more probable. Two years after the year the book was released, I would decide I wanted to live, but back then, I was not ready. At age fifteen, I had my first suicidal thought, but it wouldn't be the last. I didn't want to live in my disabled body. I am aware now that this is what people expect of disabled people and their bodies, and so, in many ways, I was feeding into outside expectations: the disabled girl who wanted to die because she craved what she thought was normalcy, a fighting chance at happiness and love that she believed wasn't possible in a body with cerebral palsy. I believed so deeply that I could not have happiness, joy, or romantic love that death felt like the only option. I wanted silence, if even for a moment. Refuge from the self-hate I both loathed and nurtured. After all, it had the top bunk, the seniority, and the final say. I gave it the ability to turn a good day or moment into a bad one with little reminders of things that don't really matter now and should have never mattered. I grew comfortable with it, relished its familiarity and gave it space to grow, to fester and tether itself to me so I felt lost without the constant barrage of insults and disgust I shot toward myself. I called myself the names I was convinced people were calling me behind my back. I saw my body pass by in mirrors and scoffed at the dragging leg, the chubby cheeks, the big forehead, and what I saw as extra rolls of fat despite weighing 110 pounds. I told myself—as I stood with bent legs, right hand far too high in the air—that I was never going to be enough for anyone, and, more important, even for myself. I felt I deserved my sadness for being born into a body unlike that of so many other people in my life. I was insecure about my black skin, too. I loved being black; I never wanted or wished to be anything else; but I was convinced that coupled with my disability it lowered my desirability to my white and black male classmates alike. I didn't realize how unhealthy and harmful this idea was until a few years ago.

I have always believed in God. I have not always liked him. I have been angry with him and then immensely grateful for what he has given me. I used to pray for him to not wake me up in the morning, but he always did, thank . . . well, God. Sometimes, the thought, the memory, the urgency with which I spent so many years of my life wanting to die makes me laugh. The desire isn't funny, but I spent so long with that version of me that forgetting how she feels and moves, pushing her out of mind like a guest who's overstayed her welcome, is funny to me, because she was such an integral part of my life. But once I was ready and healthy enough to drop her like a bad habit, I did. I guess she was a bad habit, a bad influence, and a bad choice of confidante on my part. At once she went from the person who knew me best to the old friend you see but can't bear to speak to. The friend who hurt me so deeply that "I'm sorry" would never be enough. Cutting someone out of your life, a part of yourself who knew you so completely in your formative years, is hard regardless of the toxicity.

Still, I don't hate her as much as I did when she was here, pulling the reins of our life. I spent a lot of times resenting her because she had so much power over every aspect of my life, and while I wanted control of my own, I was afraid to be without her. Now, though, I understand why she was the way she was. She was scared, angry, and tired all the time. She wanted relief from the thoughts we created but found it only in other terrible and toxic thoughts. We were so bad for each other; we moved together like two lovers who don't love each other anymore but love the routine, the familiarity of each other. When we grew tired of each other, we simply rolled over on either side of the bed and pretended that everything was fine. But it never was. We spent our days being defensive, convinced that we were an easy target, when in fact we were the only one using our faces for target practice. She was meaner to me than anyone else could possibly be, but we decided it wasn't for the same reasons that others were going to be. We were preparing for our own future battles versus pretty girls and boys who thought these things about us, too. They never came. She was dangerous, but she was mine, she was me, and so I protected her still even when the logical side of my brain tried to intervene to tell me she wasn't good for us. In high school, we believed our body made us undatable, kept us from living out the high school experience we watched in movies every weekend. There was no time for refuge or cutting ourselves slack, not when we were constantly reminded of the way our cerebral palsy, our disabled body, made us different from everyone else. When the world treats the "other" body, your body, as a thing to detest, it's hard not to listen, not to take it to heart.

We turned on the TV and saw ourselves only in exploitive telethons or viral videos in which disabled people were treated as inspirations and tapped to make able-bodied people feel better about
the lives they had and the things their bodies allowed them to do.
We spent days switching between insulting ourselves and the people
who had it better than us. She took the reins and I let her. I was never
good at giving directions anyway. When she became toxic, so did
I. She told me lies that I was eager to believe. Lies that tricked me
into pushing away the people we loved because they didn't understand how much it hurt to be alive. She allowed me to be the ugliest
version of myself, cheered me on as I stopped trying to find joy and
let my anger and pain wash over me. I stayed with her for too long,
reveling in the comfort and routine of the wish to die and rid myself
of my body. We believed that the other, the able body, was superior.
We always saw our body as the enemy. A body with beautiful black
skin and cerebral palsy we read as the blessing versus the curse. The
blessing was the love and appreciation of black skin, to know that it
was beautiful and worthwhile even if we were not. Growing up, we
saw people with our skin being desired, loved, and confident, and for
a while, that was enough—until it wasn't.

So, I worked hard to keep my head down. I tried to prepare myself for four years of high school rejection by flirting with cute boys
with the assumption they'd never be interested in me, so when they
rejected me I could claim it was all in good fun. I did this even while
holding out hope that my life would be like that depicted in the teen
movies I loved so much. I was supposed to be the girl who, despite
her small or not-so-small faults, got the guy in the end. I gave so
much of myself to this idea that I was devastated when it didn't happen. They did not want me, so I did not want me. I struggled watching my friends date and fall in and out of love while I was just the

friend who was asked to put in a good word. I internalized the small silences in conversations with my male friends whom I didn't even have romantic feelings for and chalked them up to personal faults rather than just teenage angst. I never allowed things to get better the following year. I was too convinced that I had to stay on high alert, ready for any attacks that may come without realizing that I was the only one attacking me.

At sixteen, I typed out a will and left all my books to my sister and an apology to my mother, sister, and best friend. They never saw these notes—I deleted them all a week later after deciding I couldn't take my own life before the end of high school because I'd worked hard to get there. (I hope they never ask me what those letters said.) After deciding to wait until after graduation, I turned to books to keep me occupied. In high school, I was a big fan of all things Sarah Dessen; she is one of the reasons I write today. She makes her readers feel so much. I am no longer in her target demographic because I am in my late twenties, but I read her books anyway, the same way I did when I was younger. Through her words, Sarah makes her readers feel heard and understood without being patronizing. She writes characters I want to know and worlds I want to visit, places where I can escape to or at least find a reprieve from my depressive thoughts.

Depression and suicidal ideation do not care about effort and good days, because they know that there will always be bad ones, and those are the times and days that they thrive. Depression lies; it tells you things that you know deep down are not true, but you are desperate to believe in something and so you give it all you have. I gave it everything I had, and it left me broken and bruised. Books were my only reprieve, my only sense of true joy, aside from music for so long.

Sarah's books allowed me to be with Halley as she watched her best friend, Scarlett, grieve the loss of her boyfriend, and with her again as Scarlett found out she was pregnant with his baby. I longed for a friendship like theirs. I almost convinced myself it was possible, but the part of me that grabbed the reins on our depression and hopelessness was convincing enough to remind me otherwise. When we made it to college, leaving most of those books at home and coming out on the other side of a bad friendship breakup with our freshman-year roommate, the version of me who was hurting, that part of me who was ready and eager to hurt me and my progress, showed up to my group therapy appointments, pestering me until the group and I shooed her away by confronting her head-on. Still, she was always waiting for me outside the counseling center's doors; I pictured her sometimes in a leather jacket, jeans, and Converse sneakers, leaning up against the building with a smirk on her lips. I'd roll my eyes but let her come with me. We never talked about the brave faces I tried to put on at therapy; we didn't have to. She was in control, and she was not at all threatened even as a manifestation of my worst fears, toxic behavior, and sadness. She knew that the person I am now, who was always there, knew not to stage a coup. At least, not yet.

Though I never saw my full self in any of Sarah's characters, I was so desperate to carry a piece of their world into mine that I tried to mold my friendships into something that resembled theirs. I wanted someone outside my family to miss me when I was gone and I wasn't sure they would otherwise. I watched Annabel and Owen find one another when they needed each other most; and I watched the relationship between Remy and Dexter ignite and fizzle and ignite again and imagined that my first relationship would do the same. Sarah Dessen's books gave me a sense of hope when I was hopeless, and I will forever be thankful for them and for her because of it.

I had planned to take my life on October 12, 2009. I had had a particularly difficult day and I think my roommate was at one of her night classes. I don't quite remember now. I was going to take an entire bottle of ibuprofen, and as I sat on my bed crying and trying to prepare myself, I spotted my copy of Dessen's *The Truth about Forever* peeking out of my shelf in the corner of the room. I wiped my tears, stood up, and walked to it. I grabbed the book and held it close to my chest, remembering how I'd felt when I first read it. I decided then to read a few chapters instead of swallowing a bottle of pills, and I ended up falling asleep with the book by my pillow. The next day, my grandmother died, and I told no one about the events from the night before. Instead, I tucked the book into the overnight bag I rushed to put together to go home with the next morning. Every year since, on the day before I grieve the loss of my grandmother, I take a silent moment to read a passage from the book that stopped me from making the last decision of my life. I will keep Sarah's books forever and I will always be grateful that she put words together that allowed me to save myself. That's the magic of writing and the gift of being able to give someone the ability to see another day when all they want to see is darkness.

As I grew older, finishing out the last years of college, with the help of books, music, friends, and therapy, I felt myself drifting from my suicidal thoughts. It's never really that easy, though, is it? She didn't like that I was trying to get better, trying to prove to myself and to her that I would be okay if I tried. She had other plans, and she was comfortable and desperate to stick around. Me, I remained tired of her but felt unable to do anything about it. She was smart and fed off my exhaustion, my unwillingness to fight, and pressed herself into all my free spaces. When I'd scream at her to leave, she would go if only for a day, leaving a toothbrush or a bracelet behind for any excuse to return. She attended my classes with me, reminded me just how little I had to offer the world and the spaces I was in, and she accompanied me on nights out with friends as well, only to laugh when they got hit on and served free drinks while we just stood there wondering why we weren't good enough for the same treatment. My lack of a love life was the most useful tool in her toolbox. She kept me believing I wouldn't be able to survive without her. We lived like it was us against the world. Our anger was our defense mechanism, and we tried our best to tear us down under the guise that when someone else did it wouldn't impact us. In the few and far-between instances that someone did tear us down, it did have an impact on us, and it always affected us in the worst way.

When I finally became tired of tearing us down, using myself as a punching bag when we were the only ones who ever ended up losing, when I was finally tired enough to do something about it, I decided that maybe it was time I give myself a break. The breaks from my own thoughts were short and sporadic. Whenever I was doing something I loved, I tried to let my thoughts focus on it and not on me or the way I saw myself. Instead, I gave myself completely over to the task I was completing. When that didn't work, I always turned to one of Sarah's novels when the worst of my thoughts got too loud.

I saw so much of who I was inside and who I wanted to be in Sarah Dessen's characters. They were both confident and insecure but loved anyway. They were flawed and still beautiful, still worthy of love and affection, and somehow, despite their feeling ordinary, someone always found or saw something extraordinary in them. I wanted that so desperately when I was at my saddest and I want it now, but the difference is that now, I know I deserve it as much as the conventionally attractive people in my life and in the world.

Where I didn't see my skin in Sarah's books, I saw it in Toni Morrison's. I saw grief and love in a way I never had before. A celebration

of the two, together and apart. Black people have always found joy
and love in the worst of circumstances. But generations of oppression—for black people and other people of color—have affected the
way we view the world, and it is this perspective, and these oppres-
sions, that Morrison explores so deeply and so masterfully in her
work.

As a disabled black woman, I view the world through the lens of
what is and isn't expected or allowed of me. There are so many rules
for marginalized people yet so many expectations, too. When I first
saw the film adaptation of Morrison's *Beloved*, I was seven years old
and far too young to be anything but scared at the idea of a ghost
coming to life. When I read the book during the summer between
my sophomore and junior years of high school, I understood less of
it than I would like to admit. But what I did feel in my bones the first
time I read it, and again for the second time in college, was that it was
a masterpiece. I was transported into Sethe's world, was able, through
Morrison's genius, to see what my ancestors had to deal with. I understood why Sethe would rather her baby be dead than sold into
slavery, and I felt the pain it must have caused her. I understood then
that my pain, my depression, was valid, and I realized that I didn't
have to pretend to be happy, to be loved, because maybe the right
people would love me anyway, for who I was. In reading that book,
I understood that no one person was happy all the time and that the
complicated expression of our emotions makes the world a much
richer place. I say as much without excusing the actual trauma and
pain the characters go through, because they do not deserve it. There
is a strange phenomenon in finding comfort when you can recognize
your pain in others and realize that maybe you could find a way to
the other side of yours whether they did or did not. I would attend
my Novels and Tales class to discuss the assigned chapters, then head

straight to counseling to discuss how I related to the pain and grief, how losing my grandmother made me think again of wanting to die just to be with her, that her death meant I'd lost a part of myself and I did. I felt like half a person, half a soul. I couldn't let go of the pain, and I understood Sethe most in these moments. I told my counselor that I was desperate to feel again. I spoke of how I wanted so badly to write something that moved someone the way *Beloved* had moved me.

I let Dessen's and Morrison's books keep me here, alive, when not much else could. I read them to keep going, to give my day-to-day life meaning when I felt there was no way I could keep living under the weight of my depression and grief. Chapter by chapter and page by page I got through days and months because I needed to get to the happy ending. I needed to see if I could have my own. Every book that has helped me get to where I am has had a happy ending or a resolution that made me feel okay. Those two books, *Beloved* and *The Truth about Forever*, were my haven, and now they are my reminders—my reminders that if I keep working at my happiness I do not have to ever be who I was again. I turn to these books and others when I am at my lowest (and highest), as reminders of how far I've come and how far I must go. The journey won't be easy, but it will be worth it. That's the real magic of books, how they move and change us, and how they can save us from ourselves.

We became *I* on December 28, 2016, when I left my depression and suicidal thoughts with her cutting words, hatred, and power over me on the bathroom floor, as I looked in the mirror and complimented the person looking back at me for the first real time in my life. After that day, I made a conscious effort to say something nice about myself every morning and night. Thinking back on that day, I see that the decision to try was what made it stick. Initially I believed that she would be back again in the morning after a few hours of peace. She'd wake me up laughing at how naive I was to think she could be dismissed so easily. However, in the morning she was not there, and the next day and the next and the next. In her place were cuter outfits, bolder hairstyles, a genuine smile, a viral hashtag, and a promise to live and try in the face of adversity and the face of success. The hashtag #DisabledAndCute was created in February 2017 as a way for me to celebrate my newfound and unapologetic joy in my body. The hashtag went viral on Twitter, Facebook, Instagram, and Tumblr, with features in *Teen Vogue*, *Cosmo*, Yahoo!, and more, but this is not an essay about the hashtag. This is an essay about living when you spent so long wanting to die.

So, how do you do it? How do you live when you want to die? For starters, you search for patience. You'll need it to deal with yourself on the days that leave you questioning your decision to try. You'll need it when you fight the reflex to criticize the roundness of your face and the way your stomach folds when you sit and when you stand. Patience will keep you when your knees give out and you curse your body for causing you pain. Patience is necessary for setbacks, and there will be setbacks, days when you can't get out of bed or remember only how easy it is to become that mean, sad, and angry person again, when night falls and you spend hours thinking about all the embarrassing things that have happened to you. Patience will be there to fondly roll its eyes and tell you to go to bed. When you have enough patience, you'll need honesty. Honesty is imperative for continued joy. Honesty will allow you to hold yourself accountable, will force you to feel what you need to feel when you need to feel it. Honesty will give you the gift of apologizing to the people whom you've hurt in your quest to hurt yourself. You won't be able to take back the names you called them in anger and jealousy, but you can make a vow to be kinder to them every day and love them the way they love you or give them the space they desire, because honesty will also teach you that you are not owed forgiveness just because you ask for it. The last thing you need may take you a while to acquire, and that's love. If you're lucky, you'll have people in your life who love you enough to help you discover the things you love about yourself. They will be your guiding light as you continue your journey.

There's something magical about wanting to live after you've wanted to die. There are days, weeks, months, and years that are gone forever. That's the thing about time: it doesn't pause or stop when we want or need it to, or even at all. I can't get that time back, but what I can do is work harder to nurture the love that I have fostered and make a conscious effort to keep going even when I feel the old me sneaking back up and trying to infiltrate the new life I have now.

Love itself is a tricky thing. Love has a way of enhancing every aspect of one's life. Before I knew self-love, I was showered with familial and platonic love. After years of believing that the only love missing was romantic, I now know that the love that was missing for me to finally accept the person that I am and the body that I live in was love for myself. Romantic love would be nice—I won't lie, I yearn for it, especially as I age, sure—but at the end of the day, I get to navigate the world knowing that I'm finally okay with myself. On the days when I misplace this love, I give myself the room to feel what I believe is necessary. The road is bumpy and tiring, but being here now at twenty-seven, after twenty-four and a half years on the road to self-destruction, I know there's nowhere else I'd thrive.

I won't tell you that my life is a happy ending tied up with a cute blue bow. I am still messy, literally and emotionally, but I am working to make my life one I feel is worth living every single day. I feel like I am hitting my stride; I found my purpose, and the work I do matters to others as much as it matters to me. There are moments when I think of her, of the person I was, and the thoughts of her and who I was fuel me to make sure that no one else feels the way I once did, if I can help it. When I have bad days now, it is not for the same reasons my bad days were before. My body is not in the limelight, under investigation or scrutiny, and that has been quite the adjustment. My frustration often lies in situations and things, not me. The relief of that is so exciting. In my saddest moments, I am lonely. I want to be loved romantically and I think I deserve it. Still, if something goes wrong, it is not through the fault of my existence, which feels wild in a way I cannot explain. I am not the sole reason for something being amiss in my life; my disability is not the reason for late starts, torn clothes, impending deadlines, or fleeting bad thoughts. Every time I say that, it feels like a celebration. Maybe it is, and maybe it should be. Life isn't perfect—I shed the idea of being healed from depression and suicidal ideation. Instead, I am working at happiness, genuinely trying to live a life that first, I am proud of, and second, that gives back to others and allows other people to see me and read my work and say to themselves, "I want to try to live, too. I want to work at being kinder to myself and finding things about me worth loving as I grow to love and respect others."

The most amazing thing about my life now is that my own view of myself, the black disabled girl from the town no one knows the name of, has changed. I like me so much that when I think about it, I giggle like I've got a crush. When I smile it feels like the sun is filling up in my body so that when I move around the world, I can light it up. I like me so much now that I know I don't need to be the best or the prettiest person anyone meets, I just need to be me, and that's enough. The world at large is still clinging to ableist and harmful ideas of disabled people. Still, I can't allow myself to let the opinions of a culture influence my whole view the way they did before. I have too much left to do and I have worked too damn hard to get here. The rest of the world will catch up whether it wants to or not. Especially with the work that the disability community, and especially the women in our community, are doing to ensure that it is happening through hell or high water.

Outside of my disability work, I want to write books that mean as much to me as Dessen's and Morrison's do. I want my future books to be a light for someone. The reason that they make it through one more year and then the next, and the next and so on. I want to spread hope and joy and tell the stories of fellow messy and complicated people. I want to lead the fight to stop killing disabled characters in fiction and entertainment. There are so many people and readers like me hurting right now, and books can be their salvation the way they are mine. I think we all deserve something that reminds us we are worthy of a life to live.

Books, music, friends, writing, television shows, delicious food, and better movies were and are the reason I am here today. I survived, and I'm still surviving because I can go in and out of worlds, fall in and out of love with characters who feel real, who know pain, characters who can get to the other side in the same way that I did with blood, sweat, and tears. I am surviving because I am loved, maybe not romantically yet, but loved nevertheless. I am surviving because of music from bands like Paramore and artists like Demi Lovato. I am surviving because I fight for what I believe in and I don't let my own fears get in the way. The saying goes, "It takes a village." And it does—the only difference is I did not know I had a village to call my own.

As I sit and write these words, I have never been more thankful for the fact that I am still here on earth. Don't worry, I realize how cheesy that sounds, but I mean it. The truest form of joy is waking up on the other side of suicidal ideation and discovering truths that you never thought were possible. The other side for me is writing essays for dream publications and being an entertainment journalist writing about shows I love. The other side is solo dance parties, showing a little skin, and smiling at myself in those store mirrors; it is being assertive and confident, saying no and yes when I want to and telling myself the truth. The other side is finally seeing the potential in myself that my friends and family have seen for so long. I am not just a black woman with a disability; there is so much more to me, and that part of who I am is just a beautiful piece of the puzzle, the bigger picture. I am the pop-culture-obsessed, TV-loving, writer/journalist, cheesecake-, pizza-, and cheeseburger-eating me, and I am not only enough, but I am something special. We all are—say it with me: "I am something special." Write it on a Post-it and stick it to your mirror and then say it every morning and night until you believe it and some more after you believe it. Trust me, it helps, and at some point, you will be so used to saying it that you won't remember what life was like before you were saying it and thinking it throughout your day. Let the phrase get stuck in your head like your favorite song. You can thank me later.

There are truths about me that I had never believed before when I was too busy hating myself, truths such as the fact that my unfiltered happiness is beautiful, my ears are small and cute, and I am worthy of the love given to me. There are truths that deep down I refused to believe simply because they scared me. Truths like, I hurt people, but I am not that same person anymore, and it doesn't excuse it, but I don't have to beat myself up for it; I can grow from it. The biggest truth I have learned to accept is that normal doesn't exist. The people we idolize on TV, film, and on magazine covers are beautiful, but they don't always look so put together and perfect. We are all just trying to get along in the best way we know how. We should try our best to help each other along the way.

When you spend so long tearing yourself down, you realize that lifting yourself back up and believing in the natural talent you have in the career you have chosen is petrifying. That's probably why it took me so long. I am good at what I do, and it took falling in love with myself to admit that. Self-love stopped the self-deprecating jokes (most of them, anyway), the debilitating anger and doubt, and the crushing weight of sadness. Self-love gave me reasons to deal with the days, weeks, and months when depression found me again instead of letting them consume me. For the first time in my life, I see the other side, and it is perfect for me. I didn't die when I wanted to, and I wanted to for almost all my life, but something bigger stopped it from happening: I stopped it from happening. I always believed that someone else was meant to save me like they save the beautiful girls in the movies that I love, but in saving myself I learned not only to love the person I am saving but also to let her grow. I didn't die when I wanted to, and I wanted to for almost all my life, but if I had gone through with it, I wouldn't be where I am today, and where I am today is the best place for me to be.

I want so many things in life now, things that I never thought possible. They may never come to be, but I am shooting for the stars anyway. I want to be in conversation with Oprah for her SuperSoul Conversations, and I want to be on *Ellen* and in the writers' room of a Shondaland TV show. I want to write so many books and travel the world. I dream of writing a movie and acting in one. I dream of seeing disabled black girls in mainstream media being told that we are beautiful, too. As much as I dream of these things, I will work even harder because dreams are the first step, but the work is what makes it reality. I am not the first disabled black woman to tell her story. I may simply be one of the first whose book you've read, but I promise not to be the last.

In 2018, I went to a purpose party at my sister's youth group. The speaker swore that we would be forever changed. I thought he was laying it on a little thick, truly, but here is what I know now: I was put on this earth to help people feel good about themselves, to see their worth and importance, to help people see that different is not only beautiful but important and not only important but motivating. I tell stories and put words together for a living, and I love it. Whenever I am asked how I became a writer I tell the story of my high school English teacher encouraging me to give it a shot. The story is true. However, I was always a writer. I wrote songs and poems as a young girl about boys who would never like me back. You are a writer when you write, but the only difference between the writer that I was then and the writer I am now is that I believe my work is worthy of the audience I am building. We don't have a lot of control in our lives. We like to think we do, but we don't. What we can control is the energy we put out into the world, the way we view ourselves. I won't pretend it is easy. I won't lie and tell you that I do not still struggle, but I am trying, and to try in the face of the familiar and deceiving bad thoughts is worth celebrating. Remember that when you embark on a journey of your own. If you are trying your hardest, you are doing the best you can with what you can.

I love myself now. I love every inch of my body. I love every scar from surgeries to the ones acquired when I lost my balance. Every fold, crease, bump, and bruise. When I walk in public with my limp and bent fingers, I do so with confidence and pride in the body that may not look like everyone else's but matters just the same. I had no control over what my body would look like or how I'd react to it when I was brought into life. I am sure that's why I spent so long hating myself and my body because I didn't understand it, but I am learning more every single day. I did not have a choice in the hardships that would come with disability—and there are plenty—but my friends, amazing taste in music, career path, and interests are in my control, so why shouldn't I share them with the world?

The path to getting here was long and hard. I still have bad days when I can feel myself slipping back into unhealthy habits, opening the door to let her in, but now I know how to catch myself before I slip, and I shut the door before she can step inside. I had to learn how to be kinder to myself, and I must remember that I am a human who can be susceptible to the ease of my sadness. To combat that, I need to continue learning how to exchange the negative thoughts about what I do and don't have in comparison with other people for reminders that there are wonderful things about me as well. Every single day isn't a bed of roses. I'm not fixed or free entirely of my depression, but I haven't had a suicidal thought in four years, and I am genuinely trying for the first time in my life—and that has got to count for something. I have an enthusiastic sense of humor; I think that I am hilarious even when I am the only one laughing at my jokes. Couple that with a boisterous laugh, a bright smile, an urge to talk to people, a love of cute and sophisticated clothes I do not have the funds for, and a desire to create things that matter. I am loyal to the people I care about, I care too much about what people think, I am quick-tempered, and I procrastinate even while being prolific due to the fear that it will all be snatched from me in the dead of night. Nevertheless, I am happy, and I want my people and the world to be happy, the happy that took me a long time to reach. I won't pretend it is as easy as saying the words, because every day and every life is different and comes with its own set of unique challenges, but I don't want anyone to feel the way that I did.

The thing is, I don't love just my physical body. I love the person I am becoming. A person who works hard for what she wants, who writes about her black skin, disability, and feminism without apology. A person who finally understands her value and believes that with a lot of vigorous work, a little luck, and the right timing, all her dreams are possible, and I am so thankful for that. In telling these stories and revealing aspects of my life that have made me uncomfortable, I hope that they help people tell stories of their own and be a little more lenient and kind to themselves in the process. There is so much more to me than meets the eye, and the journey that I am on and the life that I am living is worth it even on the worst days, because it feels damn good to be alive.

ACKNOWLEDGMENTS

There are many people who have gotten me to this very page. My family: my mother, Cheryl; sister, Leah; aunts: Regina, Renee, and Michele; uncles: Scottie, Mikey, and Terry; and lastly, cousins: Jeremy, Meesha, Kaylee, Mykele, Melaine, and Mahogony. Thank you for loving me first. This would not have been possible without you.

Thank you to Trident Media Group. A special thank-you to Alex Slater, my wonderful agent who saw something in me and this book before it had its name. You're the greatest. #TeamSlater

Thank you to Atria Books, who gave *The Pretty One* a home. Jhanteigh Kupihea, who acquired this book and made my dream come true, before leaving me in Rakesh Satyal's masterful hands: thank you, I will be forever grateful. Rakesh, this book is everything I ever hoped it would be—you are an amazing editor. Thank you for taking this ride with me word for word, message for message, and page by page. Loan Le, your kindness and attentiveness make you the perfect assistant editor; thank you for everything. Thank you to my copy editor, Doug Johnson.

To my friends, you know who you are, thank you for answering my texts and understanding when deadlines meant I often couldn't answer yours. Thank you for sending me happy things when I was working on tough parts of the book and reminding me just how sappy I am. Thank you for choosing to love and know me every day. I love you back, always.

Thank you to the Lockport Public Library, where much of this collection's essays were written, added to, or finished, and the musicians whom I put on my carefully curated playlist to write this collection.

Thank you to every editor at every publication I have ever written for. Thank you for trusting me to tell my stories and the stories of others. Each essay and article helped get me here. You took chances on a black disabled woman and I have been better for it each time.

I am not in this fight alone—there are many disabled and chronically ill women/non-binary people who fight alongside me. Some include: Porochista Khakpour, Esmé Weijun Wang, Karrie Higgins, Vilissa Thompson, Alice Wong, Rebecca Cokley, Coffee Spoonie, Jillian Mercado, Lena Dunham, Kayla Whaley, Maysoon Zayid, Annie Segarra, Abby Norman, S.E. Smith, Imani Barbarin, Carly Findlay, Angel Powell, and Heather Watkins.

Finally, thank you to every reader of this book and every person on social media who believes in the work I am doing on and off of it. We can only go up from here!

ABOUT THE AUTHOR

Keah Brown is a writer, journalist, and, now, author whose work has appeared in *Harper's Bazaar*, *Teen Vogue*, *Glamour*, *Essence*, and Lenny Letter, among others. She was named one of *The Root*'s 100 Most Influential African Americans of 2018. Keah is an advocate for proper representation for people with disabilities in the media. She has dreamed about writing books her entire life and meeting Oprah. Keah hopes to one day call California home, but for now she writes from a small black desk in the home she shares with her mother, sister, and brother in western New York. Find out more at keahbrown.com, and on Twitter and Instagram @Keah_Maria.